HALFRICAN AMERICAN:

THE STRUGGLE IS REAL

Written by Wilhelm Macmay Mwengi

Dedication

This book is wholeheartedly dedicated to my cherished daughters, Riley Mwengi and Zoey Mwengi, whose unwavering presence has illuminated my path and guided me toward authenticity, perpetually reminding me of my profound responsibility as their father.

Book Summary:
Halfrican American:
The Struggle Is Real

Between Worlds: The Halfrican American Odyssey explores the unique identity of someone born in Africa and raised in the United States. Introducing the term **"Halfrican American,"** this blend of personal narrative and broader social commentary delves into the search for belonging, resilience, and self-realization. Through powerful storytelling, the book navigates the challenges of adapting to a new culture while holding onto one's roots. It emphasizes the strength found in embracing dual heritage.

The author shares personal experiences, such as dealing with **racism** and feeling caught between two worlds, making the narrative vivid and relatable. Alongside these **life challenges**, it offers lessons and inspiration, providing readers with insights into **overcoming** feelings of disconnection and discovering a path to authenticity and purpose. Are you ready to uncover the nuanced journey of an Halfrican American?

Preface

The **alligator lunged** towards me in a heartbeat, sending my heart racing and my bike skidding across the path. It was 2016, and I had traded my car for a daily **50-mile bike** commute to work through a seemingly peaceful park. This marked the start of a journey filled with adversity and self-discovery. The shift in lifestyle, ironically, contrasted sharply with my African childhood. There, long walks to school were unthreatened by wildlife. Yet, in the U.S., danger lurked in the most routine activities.

Riding into the park that day, I was caught off guard in more ways than one. Just moments after dodging the alligator, my bike spun out of control, and I crashed hard onto the gravel path. This was just one of many bike crashes that tested my resilience in unexpected ways.

These bike accidents were only part of the trials I faced. My mother's stroke, a challenging **divorce,** and the responsibility of caring for my autistic nephew converged, plunging me into a profound struggle with anxiety and depression. Sleepless nights and the weight of despair threatened to overwhelm me.

Yet, amidst the chaos, I found a steadying force in the resilience instilled during my upbringing in Kenya. Immersed in nature's rhythms and the tasks of herding cattle, I had learned patience and the interconnectedness of life. These lessons became my anchor, reminding me of the vital role of family and the strength found in **community bonds.**

In this book, I explore themes central to our shared human experience—resilience, personal growth, identity, opportunity, and finding balance. Through personal stories and reflections, I offer insights into overcoming adversity, **embracing our worth,** and building a fulfilling life.

Welcome to "**Halfrican American: The Struggle Is Real.**" Let's embark on a journey that transcends continents, delving into the heart of human endurance and spirit.

Table of Contents

Part I:
Resilience and
Overcoming Adversity

In the face of challenges, resilience and determination guide us through. These stories reveal the strength within us, turning adversity into a catalyst for growth and transformation.

"Smooth seas do not make skillful sailors."
– African Proverb

Turbulence and Triumph:
My Sky-High Journey to Resilience

Meeting Her

I saw her first, as fate often **murmurs its secrets.** She stood at the entrance, her poise captivating, the light catching the glint in her eyes. Her red lipstick perfectly accentuated her lips, just above a neatly tied **neckerchief.** My breath caught—just for a moment. Her uniform hugged her as if she had been baptized in it. **"Welcome aboard,"** she said, her smile both inviting and professional.

My adventure began in **1998 when, as a teenager**, I took my first flight to the U.S., headed to college. My heart was a mix of wonder and anxiety. I was torn between excitement for what lay ahead and the fear of the unknown. The enormity of the plane, a massive metal beast compared to the cattle I herded in my Kenyan village, left me awestruck. As I moved past the flight attendant, I carried her smile

3

with me, a **small comfort** amidst the vast unknown. Back home in Nguluni, life was simple and grounded, filled with the fresh air of rolling fields and the warmth of a close-knit community.

As I gazed out of the tiny window, the landscape of my homeland faded below, the familiar terrain **slipping away**, disappearing into the distance along with everything I'd ever known. I knew this journey would take me far from what I knew into skies that were both exhilarating and unpredictable. It felt **uprooting** as if I were being exposed, stripped naked of my **innocent teenage years.**

Isolation in the Air

On the plane, I felt a pang of isolation beneath my **false bravado.** Everything here felt foreign—the tight rows of seats, the cold blast of air from tiny vents above, and the strange hum of the engines that never seemed to stop. The cabin was filled with a sense of dead air, heavy and stagnant, a stark contrast to the open skies I was used to. When I tried to open the window for fresh air, a flight attendant's sympathetic, gentle correction left me both embarrassed and grateful. **"Those don't open,"** reminding me of the vast cultural gap I was crossing.

Finding Humor and Resilience

My stomach churned and growled from the turbulence, a wave of nausea rolling through me. As the **nausea** intensified, I couldn't help but wonder if they had **a pit latrine** like back in our village. Misunderstandings, like thinking the overhead bins were for sleeping, turned into moments of laughter and learning.

The plane jolted again, and my hand instinctively gripped the armrest. The man next to me leaned over with a half-smile, "If we crash, you won't feel a thing," he said. His words, though unsettling, reminded me that even here, miles above the earth in a metal bird I barely understood, people could still find ways to **connect**—something that felt strangely comforting in this sea of unfamiliarity.

Cultural Misunderstandings

When the flight attendant asked for my drink order, I innocently **requested porridge.** Heads turned as I inquired, "Porridge with milk, please—no sugar." The flight attendant's eyes twinkled with amusement as she stifled a laugh, perhaps wondering if this was a genuine request or if I was just trying to liven up her day. "How about some milk instead?" she winked playfully. I smiled back, but inside, I felt a deep longing for the **familiar comforts** of home—like the warm sun on my back and the sound of cattle lowing in the fields.

This starkly reminded me of the **cultural gap** I was navigating. The mix of amusement and alienation left me feeling both determined and daunted. I began to realize just how different my new world would be.

Landing and Realization

As I alighted from the plane, the flight attendant said to me, **"Good luck."** "Why do I need good luck in the land of milk and honey?" I wondered. As the airplane door closed, a bittersweet wave washed over me, mingling the excitement of the journey ahead with the poignant finality of our brief encounter. Her warm smile lingered, a fleeting kindness amid the transience of travel. Perhaps she was already preparing to embrace another village boy, reminding me that every journey is both a departure and an arrival.

The first gust of cool, conditioned air struck me. It was unlike anything I had ever felt back in the village. It felt like a strange, gentle hand brushing against my skin, grounding me in the moment. Almost unnatural. In that instant, I began to understand that the "**milk and honey**" I sought would come not just from the land but from the resilience and connections I would forge along the way. I wondered

5

if I'd find the "milk and honey" in the new land, or would it come from within me?

Stranded in Dallas

Landing in Dallas, I was immediately struck by the vastness of the airport. It **dwarfed my village,** with its endless corridors and bustling crowds. The unfamiliar Texas twang of the announcements turned each word into a puzzle, adding to my growing sense of disorientation. I searched the sea of faces for the person who was supposed to pick me up, but no one came forward.

As minutes turned into hours, I stood by a vending machine, clutching my **Kenyan shillings**—like grains of salt in a world that no longer barters, useless. They felt heavy and foreign in my hand, a cruel reminder of my mistake. My reflection stared back at me, distorted in the glass as if mocking my plight. The realization hit me like a ton of bricks.

My dreams, so vivid on the plane, now seemed distant and unattainable. The bright, artificial lights of the airport glared down, **harsh and unfeeling**. Once so vibrant, my hope now flickered dimly like a dying ember. I watched travelers reuniting with loved ones; their laughter and embraces were a painful reminder of my own **isolation**. As the day turned into night, the airport began to empty, and the bustling crowds thinned out. It became painfully clear that **my ride was never coming.**

I sank onto a hard plastic bench, my suitcase beside me, and fought back tears. The fear of being **abandoned** in a foreign land gripped me, my mind racing with confusion. What was I to do? Where could I go? There were no phones back in my village to call someone. The immensity of my situation felt crushing, and I longed for the comforting familiarity of home.

Suddenly, the flight attendant's wish of good luck echoed in my mind, her words now prophetic. Abandoned at the airport, I felt a wave of **panic and loneliness** wash over me, stronger than ever before. I wondered if she and her neckerchief thought of me and the journey I was undertaking.

Harambee Spirit

By a stroke of luck, I overheard someone speaking **Kiswahili,** and he approached me.

"Are you stuck too?" he asked with a knowing smile, a hint of sympathy in his eyes. "No worries, it's common here. Come on, I'll give you a ride."

His offer filled my heart with gratitude. It brought a sudden, unexpected warmth. Even in the most **unfamiliar places,** human kindness can bridge the gap between loneliness and belonging. At that moment, amid the turbulence of being in a foreign land, this simple act felt like an anchor, grounding me. It offered solace.

Lessons Learned

These experiences, from the turbulence in the air to the challenges on the ground, taught me the value of humor and resilience. I realized that even during **turbulence,** the pilot doesn't stop mid-air; they trust the journey, and so should we when faced with life's turbulence. Despite the fear and uncertainty, each step forward was a step toward growth.

This reminds us that we must let go of our comforts and trust the journey ahead, keeping an open mind to explore, learn, and grow— whether through embarrassing moments or humorous ones. Reflecting on these moments, I understand that life, like a flight, is filled with turbulence.

Taking Flight

Are there "flights" you've been avoiding? What action can you take today to bring you closer to boarding your "flight?" Taking a flight might mean going for that job despite its challenges or moving to a place with more opportunities.

Remember Erin Hanson's words: **"What if I fail?** Oh, but darling, what if you fly?" Let this remind you that the possibility of soaring far outweighs the fear of falling. Take that step and embrace the uncertainty—you might just discover how high you can go.

For me, taking a flight meant moving to a new continent without knowing anyone. It was **terrifying**, but it led to incredible opportunities and personal growth. Whatever your **"flight"** may be, taking that leap can open doors to unexpected and amazing destinations. So, take that step today, and who knows—you might just find yourself soaring higher than you ever imagined.

Beyond the Beer Freezer: Pursuing Dreams Against All Odds

The Cold Start

Imagine **stocking beer** in a frigid gas station room, the icy air biting at your fingers, each shiver a testament to your determination. In 1999, my journey in the U.S. began there, a cold awakening far from my dreams. Bundled up in extra clothes from the beer freezer, I often relied on Houston's unreliable bus system, sometimes **mistaken for destitute**.

The city's weather extremes—chilly frostbite in winter and oppressive humidity in summer—were a stark contrast to the savannahs' tempered climate. Wrapped in those extra clothes, I wore the **ugliness of American struggle** and adaptation.

Balancing Goals

Despite the challenges, I never lost sight of my goals. Surrounded by beer and responsibilities, I remembered my dad back in Kenya. **I owed** him for the air ticket to the U.S. Hunger emphasized the balance between immediate needs and long-term goals. Through it all, I continued to attend classes, determined to persevere through every obstacle, not to fall behind or face my **dad's wrath.**

A Lifeline

A job fair felt like a lifeline, breaking the monotony and offering new opportunities. At this job fair, I found a position in a **mailroom,** which marked a step forward from the gas station. The change came with mixed emotions—relief at moving forward coupled with anxiety about **new responsibilities** and unknown challenges.

After weathering the storm of my first struggles, getting a job in the mailroom felt like a new beginning. I was **hungry** to earn my keep. While others avoided moving boxes for HR, scared of the strict dress code and formal vibe, I saw a chance to meet new people and broaden my horizons. An attitude opportunity. With my **three pairs of pants** and three polo shirts, I didn't worry about the dress code—I embraced it.

Transition to Clerical

Because of the beer stench clinging to my clothes and my bloodshot eyes, I became the "**alcoholic**" joke among colleagues. It stung every time I heard their laughter, knowing that, in reality, I was sacrificing sleep and sanity as a "**workaholic**."

After six months in the mailroom, I applied for a clerical job but failed the typing test. Frustration clawed at my insides. I felt like **a loser,** as if I wasn't good enough and that moving boxes was all I was destined to do. Every day felt like another **step backward,** a cycle I couldn't break.

One day, while delivering boxes to HR, I discovered a **typing test computer** tucked away in the corner of the room. This was my ticket to a clerical job. My heart raced with excitement and anxiety. Mingled with a renewed sense of determination, I knew I had never practiced typing before, but I hoped this could be my chance to prove myself. It was time for my fingers to find their dance.

Learning to Type

Practicing typing with clumsy fingers was daunting, especially with some coworkers' **discouraging words:**

"It'll take you forever to learn to type."

Some days, my typing was so bad that I just felt like settling for moving boxes. Remembering herding cattle in Kenya kept me going. With no relatives around to fall back on, there was **no backup plan.** Each keystroke felt like a battle between hope and failure. Every letter typed was another step on a **fraying tightrope.** One wrong move, and it could all unravel.

How do you keep going when failure feels imminent?

Small Victories

When the screen acknowledged my input, it was a quiet triumph—a significant step toward new skills. The soft click of the keys, the faint glow of the monitor—each detail seemed to echo the significance of this step forward. Each small victory brought me closer to my dreams and helped me reduce **my debt** to my dad. Routine tasks became milestones in my growth. The words of an HR leader, "What is hard today will soon be easier," reminded me to trust my abilities.

Climbing the Ladder

My journey began in the freezer, moved through the mailroom, and eventually reached clerical support. Today, I work in HR and lead an outreach program, attending job fairs and helping others find opportunities that once helped me **transform** my life. Each step underscored the power of small beginnings and continuous learning. By embracing **mundane tasks**, I unlocked new skills and unforeseen paths, each building toward greater success. I learned that, often, you don't need advice; you just need to **trust yourself** more.

Lessons Learned

Being **judged as destitute** and called a workaholic didn't stop me. In fact, it only strengthened my resolve. I never felt the need to explain myself to those who couldn't see the bigger picture. These experiences taught me an important lesson: when you're busy chasing your dreams, **people will judge** you for everything but your drive. It's a strange irony.

The **temptations of beer** and the siren call of an easy night's sleep were constant tests of my commitment. Each time I turned them down, it was a small victory, a tangible reminder of the sacrifices I was making today for the promise of tomorrow. My grandfather's words often echoed in my mind: "Excellence isn't being the best; it's doing your best." His advice became my compass, guiding me through each challenge.

Paying Back

Paying back my dad was never truly about the money; it was about the pressure that kept me grounded and driven. That debt was more than just about repayment; it was about the motivation to **rise** above my circumstances and **fulfill my potential.** Now, armed with these lessons, I am always ready to tackle even greater challenges and to encourage others to do the same.

Final Thoughts

Remember, you might not be where you want to be, but you're also not where you used to be. What are some "boxes" in your life you might be avoiding lifting? What tasks do your colleagues avoid that you know you can handle? These tasks might just be the **"test"** you need to pass for your next big achievement. **Embrace** them. Tackle them head-on. You may find they are the stepping stones to your greatest successes.

*"Some people will never like you because
your spirit irritates their demons."*
–Denzel Washington

Texas-Sized Insults:
Rise Above with Inner Peace

A Morning Encounter

Feeling optimistic one crisp morning, I stopped at a gas station to get my usual taco and coffee on my way to work. A monster truck hogged the parking spot, its tires towering like a giant, blocking my driver's door—a stark reminder that in Texas, everything is big.

After managing to squeeze out of the car, I tried to walk in, only to find two men from the truck blocking my path. Their bloodshot eyes and the stench of **alcohol** suggested they were just starting their day. One was wearing a torn leather jacket, hinting at a rough lifestyle.

"Excuse me," I said, trying to keep my tone polite.

"This is not your house," the taller one snapped, his voice rough and unfriendly.

Choosing Self-Control

A wave of **rage** surged through me, quickening my pulse and making my head throb with heat. I took a deep breath, confronted with the gravity of the decision. I hesitated. **Retaliating** would only pull me into their negativity, **compromising** my integrity and peace of mind. My hands trembled with unspent anger, but I chose to walk away. Despite my efforts to **disengage**, their tirade continued, a storm I refused to be drawn into.

"Yeah," the shorter man sneered, **"foreigners.** Can't drive, can't park."

The taller one added with a smirk, "Move your black ass out of the way."

I clenched my fists. I'd had enough. Trying to keep my voice steady, I asked, "What's your problem?"

The shorter man spat, "Go back to your country and learn how to park!"

Ironically, it was their parking skills that needed intervention. Suddenly, I heard a loud laugh from behind. I turned, startled, and saw a **Black lady**, elegantly dressed in a business suit, likely on her way to work. Her laughter wasn't at the absurdity of the situation; it was directed at me.

She smirked and said, "These foreigners never learn, do they?"

I flinched as her words cut deeper than the **men's insults**. The realization hit me: even those who share your racial background might not empathize with your struggles if they perceive you as an outsider.

16

I felt a wave of isolation and vulnerability, but I chose to walk away despite their continued tirade. Now I was fed on bitterness.

Seeking Support

As I braced myself for more confrontation, a wave of ease swept through me when a **constable** casually walked past us into the gas station, oblivious to the situation. Desperate for **support**, I approached him, but his dismissive response left me feeling abandoned: unless I was physically harmed, he could do nothing.

My breath caught in my throat, and a cold shiver ran down my spine as the weight of his words sank in. The indifference of those meant to protect us underscored a harsh truth: **justice** is not always available when you need it most. I felt let down by the law, adrift and forsaken. A blade turned inward.

Finding Inner Peace

Reflecting on the incident, I realized the **true victory** lay in preserving my **self-respect** and not letting others' negativity affect me. Disheartened and frustrated, I returned to my car, contemplating how self-reliance fosters strength and **inner peace**. When people are rude, harsh, critical, or argumentative, recognize it's not really about you and resist the urge to react emotionally.

If a stranger tries to fight you, walk away. There is no reason to fight just because someone challenged you. **Fight** for what you believe in, something other than your pride. You can try to talk the person down if you can't walk away, but the best way to stop a fight is to not participate in one.

That evening, I wrote everything down, read it out loud, and burned the paper to stop the words from endlessly **replaying** in my mind. By voicing my emotions, I transferred them from my heart to my tongue, releasing the weight they carried. It was crucial to let the **emotions** flow through my words to purify my inner state truly.

This encounter was a harsh reminder of the deep-seated **prejudices** that still exist, but it also reinforced my belief in the strength of self-restraint and the importance of maintaining my dignity. This act underscored a universal truth: inner peace is ours to command, unaffected by others' actions. However, I realized just burning the paper wasn't enough; the incident had jarred me deeply.

The harassment I endured, coupled with the constable's indifferent presence, made it even harder to move on. I needed more concrete strategies to manage my emotions and maintain my peace. Drawing from my experience, I turned to several **techniques:**

Drawing from my experience, I turned to several techniques to help me manage my emotions:

1. **Deep Breathing**: I practiced walking while focusing on deep breaths, inhaling slowly through my nose and exhaling through my mouth. This helped clear my mind and reduce stress by increasing oxygen flow to the brain and promoting relaxation.

2. **Humming the "OM" Chant**: Softly humming the "OM" chant provided a sense of tranquility and focus, as the vibration of the sound can have a calming effect on the nervous system.

3. **Cold Baths**: Invigorating cold baths helped regulate my emotions and reset my nervous system by stimulating the **vagus nerve**, which plays a key role in mood regulation.

4. **Destructotherapy**: Visiting a rage room provided a physical outlet for releasing pent-up emotions and stress, allowing me to process anger and frustration in a controlled environment.

Final Thoughts

Implementing these strategies has been a journey in itself, filled with its own challenges and rewards. Reflecting on my progress, I realized that **healing is personal** and may take time to feel fully at peace. Now, when faced with similar situations, I remind myself of that morning's scenario, take a deep breath, and compose myself.

Remember, instead of **drinking it away,** smoking it away, eating it away, or running from it, sit with it. Healing happens by feeling.

Sometimes, the biggest victories are found not in the **battles we fight** but in the peace we choose to preserve. Inner peace is your strongest shield against the chaos of the world.

It took me years to overcome my **trauma,** and even now, the sight of that gas station serves as a stark reminder of how deeply past wounds can linger. Recently, I stopped there on my bike, hoping to clear away any lingering evil spirits—or at least grab a breakfast taco for old times' sake. I kept my **bike helmet** on, just in case—because you never know.

So, what would you do **in my shoes?** What's your go-to plan when confronted by strangers? How do you maintain your inner peace in the face of adversity?

May you find the **courage** to preserve your peace, no matter the storms.

> *"What defines us is how well we rise after we fall."*
> – Zig Ziglar

Weevils and Rugby Falls:
A Lesson in Rising & Falling

Endurance Training

During my high school years in Kenya, the absence of a gym forced us into unconventional workouts, like carrying classmates on our shoulders for a 100-yard dash. Latecomers had to carry heavier partners, intensifying the challenge and **reinforcing our resilience**. The sun scorched our bony frames, sweat streaming as we struggled through practice. Our starved bodies barely **endured**; each faltering step echoed the harsh rhythm of our African boarding school. This was the real survival series before it became a thing. A place I likened to a **penitentiary,** where you were sent to endure, overcome, and transform.

Unconventional Meals

As the rugby captain, I led a group of **determined misfits** who couldn't make it in other sports. Our meals of boiled maize with "extra protein" **weevils**, beans, and cabbage reminded us daily of our resilience. My knees jutted out like rugged peaks breaking through the earth, and my elbows sharpened as if forged into the keen edges of a bayonet from the game's physical demands. I remember one teammate joking, "If we can eat this, we can face anything!"

Those weevil-laden meals taught us to find strength and patience in **adversity**, much like weevils quietly tending the soil, preparing us for the greater fields of life. Truly, the struggle was real, embodying the essence of boarding school life. These experiences with **scarcity** and challenge underscored a crucial lesson: resilience is often forged in the fire of daily struggles.

Facing Adversity Together

Our resilience was **tested** not only in our diet but also in our training. Our first training session was a mix of nervous anticipation and determination, surrounded by the smell of freshly cut grass and a symphony of rustling trees. Amidst this setting, our coach, a recent high school grad known for grit rather than speed, ordered us:

"Step forward, flop down, **get back up,** and keep going."

We stood like ancient trees, striving to absorb the **absurdity** of the request. Then Kirimi, hands akimbo, yelled, "This is **silly!**" His outburst lightened the mood, making it easier to tackle the drill.

Driven to lead by example, I hesitated, my heart pounding with the fear of **embarrassment** and the intense desire to prove myself. Attempting to demonstrate the fall, I tested our **collective humility** and adaptability. The impact on the ground was jarring. But each time I got back up, I felt a surge of resilience and a deeper understanding of our determination. It was another reminder that the struggle was real, but so was our **determination.** This drill was not just about physical endurance but also about building **mental resilience**, a key theme in overcoming life's obstacles.

Reflecting on these moments, I realized how crucial it was to face new challenges head-on, even when they seemed absurd or **intimidating**. Think about a time you were put on the spot to try something new. How did you handle it? Did you embrace the challenge or hesitate in the face of uncertainty?

Embracing Brotherhood and Growth

After 30 minutes of our unique drill and becoming the school's running joke, our coach shifted our focus from **shame** to growth with the mantra, "Out here, you're not just teammates; you're brothers. When you fall, get back up." With each fall, we grew determined to rise, making falling down feel normal. Our antics didn't go unnoticed. Local villagers stopped by to peer at our **crazy drills** through the fence. Even the **local monkeys** joined laughing from up the trees—we were the circus. Real monkey business.

That year, we reached Nationals. Despite our hard work, we lost badly on the field, but our **tenacity** never wavered as we stood together, full of weevils and determination. **Defeat** stung, but the support from our schoolmates, who once laughed at our falls, turned the pain into a source of pride.

This experience reinforced that resilience is not about never failing but about how strong we rise after each fall. It reminded us not to hold a **grudge** against those who ridicule you when you're down; their laughter often stems from the same **ignorance** you might have once had. We realized that true strength lies not in avoiding failure but in rising each time we do.

Applying Lessons to Personal Adversity

Years later, the lessons from the rugby field took on new meaning when I sustained major injuries in a bike accident in the U.S. The **humbling** weevils of my past gave way to the fast food of the present, yet the mantra of resilience—"Get back up"—remained unchanged until I was fully recovered.

Embrace the Mantra

Embrace "get back up" as more than a **mantra**; let it define your approach to life's challenges. Remember, your life is always trying to teach you something: When life is hard, it's showing you what is broken, trying to **wake you up**. When life is good, it highlights what's working and what you need more.

There is always a lesson, connection, redirection, or opportunity for growth. Pay attention to these lessons. Face each obstacle, learn from every fall, and persistently move forward, stronger each time. Seeking support when needed is a crucial part of resilience, highlighting the strength found in community and **interdependence.**

Practical Steps to Get Back Up

1. **Do something you've never done before:** Stepping out of your comfort zone can spark new energy and perspectives.

2. **Be accountable to someone:** Sharing your goals and progress with a friend or mentor can provide motivation and support.

3. **Brighten your room:** A clean and inviting space can improve your mood and productivity.

4. **Write a letter to your future self:** This might seem unusual, but writing a letter to your **future self** can provide clarity and motivation. Detail your current struggles, aspirations, and the steps you're taking to overcome challenges. Seal it and set a date to open it in the future. This act of self-reflection can be incredibly empowering. When you write down something, you **externalize** it. This process takes the goal from abstract

thought in your mind to a **concrete form** outside of yourself, making it feel more real and attainable.

Reflect and Rise

Even if you feel like the local circus as you dust yourself off, remember that it's all part of the journey—because every stumble, no matter how public, brings you closer to your comeback.

Are you currently down and hesitant to **dust yourself** off? Reflect on a recent minor challenge and how it could be preparing you for bigger ones ahead.

Remember, if you fall down, pick something up while you're down there. Every setback is a setup for a **bounce back.** Embrace the lessons in every stumble and let each fall propel you forward.

Life's true strength lies not in never falling but in rising each time we do.

Summary:

In the face of daunting challenges and seemingly insurmountable obstacles, resilience emerges as our greatest ally. The stories shared here illustrate the profound strength that lies within each of us, waiting to be discovered and harnessed. Through perseverance and unwavering determination, we learn that adversity is not the end but a catalyst for growth and transformation.

Part II:
Growth Through Emotional Intelligence, Relationships, and Habit Change

True growth arises from understanding our emotions, building strong relationships, and **cultivating positive habits.** This section explores how these key elements shape our journey toward a more fulfilling life.

"Being challenged in life is inevitable;
being defeated is optional."
– Roger Crawford

Shift Gears with Mom:
Steering Through Life's Turns Together

A New Beginning

Have you ever been thrust into responsibilities that felt overwhelming? For me, it happened during my college years in the US. My **mom** joined me from Kenya and we began a new chapter together in a modest apartment. A **dramatic shift** from our life in Kenya. Here, everything felt different. Quieter. The walls seemed to close in around us, the silence almost suffocating. I was navigating a foreign land, balancing the weight of my studies and the new reality of being the primary support for my mom and myself.

Adjusting to Change

The first weeks were a jumble of unspoken tensions and missed routines. We stumbled through the **awkward dance** of rearranging our lives, often stepping on each other's toes. The air was thick with uncertainty as we tiptoed around each other, trying to find a new **rhythm** in a space that felt both foreign and familiar.

Back home in Kenya, conversations were scarce; as children, we followed **orders** rather than engaging in dialogues. Suddenly, I was navigating not just my life but ours, managing dating and conversations we'd never had before.

One evening, as I sat on the edge of the bed with my girlfriend Muthoni—whose name ironically means "in-law"—she whispered,

"I don't want to cause any issues with your mom. Maybe I should move out. You know we can't keep living together without my family expecting a **dowry."**

Her words hung heavily in the air. They mingled with my own unspoken fears. A week later, she moved out. Watching her pack her things, I felt a mix of guilt and relief; realizing this decision, though **painful,** marked a turning point in how I approached our new life together. It was a tough lesson in balancing relationships and responsibilities in my early twenties. However, it made me realize that sacrifices are sometimes necessary for growth and harmony.

As the days turned into weeks, we slowly began to find our footing. The initial shock and turbulence gave way to a cautious **acceptance**. As we settled into our new routine, I noticed my mom's unwavering determination to adapt.

Yet, in the midst of this adjustment, I couldn't shake the odd feeling of renewed **freedom**—it felt weird going to see my girlfriend without having to ask for permission. The autonomy was both liberating and unsettling, a reminder of the shifts in our relationship and the new dynamics we were navigating together.

Embracing Opportunities

Despite the challenges at her age, she eagerly **embraced** new opportunities. She faced each day with the same determination she once showed running her successful hair salon back in Kenya. Our early struggles began to transform into shared experiences, and slowly, a new chapter of **growth** and opportunity opened up. Back in Kenya, she owned a successful **hair salon**. Now, she worked at a local salon and had enrolled in college to further her education. It felt odd giving her pocket money, almost like stealing from a church.

"It's funny being older than my teachers," she'd chuckle, her humor shining through the challenges. "I'm learning not to wait for extraordinary opportunities but to seize **common occasions** and make them great," she often said, embodying the quote by Orison Swett Marden. Her resilience reminded me that change, no matter how difficult or at what age, could be the gateway to growth.

Bonding on the Road

Over time, I naturally became **her chauffeur**. In the car's early morning warmth, our conversations ranged from serious discussions to lighthearted banter. The sun would just be peeking over the horizon, casting a golden glow inside the car.

"Why do we always leave so late?" she'd complain.

"Don't worry, we'll be fine," I'd assure her.

As we sat in traffic, she'd often remark, "There are so many cars here; it's like a vegetable market. I can't wait to get mine."

31

Marveling at the constant stream of cars, she'd wonder aloud, **"Why are people always in their cars?"**

The sheer scale of everything surprised her. "You mean I can't walk to the market?" she'd ask, taken aback by the sprawling distances.

Each of these moments, filled with humor and astonishment, helped bridge the **gaps** between us. These drives became our sanctuary—a space for bonding and mutual understanding, punctuated at times by **awkward silences** that spoke as much as our conversations.

A Leap Towards Independence

One day, after a year of saving and searching, she handed me the keys to her new used car.

"You did what?" I exclaimed, unable to believe she bought a used car like picking tomatoes at a grocery store. Seeing the pride in her eyes, I realized this was more than just a purchase.

"So, you can drive?" I asked. "No," she answered with a determined glint, **"but you'll teach me how,"** a subtle order that contrasted with the commands I was used to back home.

I was relieved later when I found out she had bought it from a good friend. She had secretly saved her money by working at a local salon. Each dollar symbolized more than just mobility; it represented her **adaptability.** She bought her used car before she even learned how to drive, showing her ambition of not waiting for things to happen but making them happen.

This bold step not only demonstrated her **courage** but also her unwavering determination to carve out her own path. I had no choice but to start giving her driving lessons after work. Our new routine became a journey of **shared learning** and support.

Lessons on the Road

"Do I really need to learn parallel parking?" she'd grumble some days, her frustration mirroring the broader challenges we all face.

"Yes, Mom, unless you plan on leaving the car in the middle of the street," I'd joke, trying to lighten the mood.

Each driving lesson was a small **victory.** Parallel parking symbolized our challenges—testing patience, precision, and **trust**. With each lesson, we both learned the importance of patience and resilience.

As we navigated the streets, her **success** with each maneuver symbolized broader victories. "I taught you well," she would beam after mastering a particularly tricky parallel park, her playful words gently ribbing my role as the teacher.

Our light-hearted banter did more than fill the car; it **mirrored** our growth—her growing **confidence** filled the air, much like a car smoothly gliding into a parking spot, perfectly aligned and assured. A sense of triumph permeated the car. Each challenge we faced, no matter how small, taught us patience and resilience, steering us closer to independence and growth.

Transformative Journey

Buying the car was **transformative.** It enhanced her independence and opened doors to personal growth. I watched her drive away for the first time, the tires rolling forward with a quiet resolve, the road ahead wide open and inviting. An empty canvas for her to paint her ambitions. The engine revved with determination, mirroring her own ambitions. It dawned on me that our sessions were more than just lessons in driving—they were stepping stones to her **autonomy** and a shift in our relationship. She reminded me, "I've learned that what will mess you up most in life is the picture in your head of how it is supposed to be."

Inspired by Courage

Our journey together taught me the importance of navigating through life's challenges—not just to **control direction** but to make decisions that shape our destiny. Sometimes you might feel like you're parallel parking your life by going in **reverse or feeling stuck.** But remember, even then, you still have the power to guide your path and choose the direction you want to go.

My mom's journey reminded me that you're not too old, and it's never too late. And when you feel discouraged, be thankful when you don't know something, for it gives you the opportunity to learn. Inspired by my mother's courage, I encourage you to seize your opportunities now. Take **bold steps** towards your goals, even if you feel unprepared. Grab the steering wheel of your life and drive towards your future with conviction.

Drawing from these experiences, here are **three steps** to help you seize opportunities;

1. **Identify Your Goal**: Clearly define what you want to achieve. Write it down, **visualize it**, and keep it in focus. Seen your goals written down can be motivating. Writing encourages mindfulness, allowing you to **reflect deeply** on your goals, why they matter to you, and what steps are needed to achieve them. This reflection can lead to greater self-awareness and better decision-making.

2. **Take the First Step**: No matter how small, take action towards your goal. It could be a phone call, an application, or even just research.

3. **Stay Persistent**: Keep pushing forward, even when faced with obstacles. Persistence is key to turning opportunities into realities.

Remember, don't be afraid **to start over.** This time, you're not starting from scratch—you're starting from experience, just as my mom did.

You're Not Alone: Life's Icy Challenges

Tragedy Strikes Twice

On a very cold day in Houston, when the city was locked under a shimmering sheet of ice, **tragedy struck** my family twice. I had just returned from the hospital, the sterile smell of antiseptics clinging to my clothes. My mom had been **hospitalized after a stroke** had taken her voice and mobility. Suddenly, I found myself caring for my nonverbal, **autistic nephew Cain**, who had been living with my mom. I was always glued to his side, especially in public, where his fascination with **women's long hair** often led him to reach out and touch.

Silent Challenges

"You should hire a maid to babysit your nephew," my close **relative** back in Africa said over the phone. I stood in disbelief, digesting the absurdity of the suggestion. Her words felt like a slap in the face, as if my efforts were invisible, my struggles mere trifles in the grand scheme of their lives. I wanted to **scream**, to make them understand the weight of the **silence** I carried. Did they not understand what I was dealing with?

Here I was, grappling with the **immense challenge** of understanding the needs of my mom, silenced by her stroke, and my nonverbal nephew, a duo silenced by **fate.** Have you ever felt completely **abandoned** or misunderstood by those closest to you, as if your struggles were invisible to the very people you hoped would understand?

The situation was deeply **ironic.** It felt as if God was weaving a silent message to me, a message I was desperately trying to decipher in a world that had gone quiet. Adding to the weight of it all, I could barely afford the mounting medical fees. Worse, I had the strain of paying both my mortgage and mom's rent. The **financial burden** was a constant shadow, a reminder of the precariousness of our situation. Dark and gloomy. And yet, each morning, I had to muster the strength to **show up for work**, pretending everything was fine while the stress gnawed at me from within. I **buried** small parts of myself under my humor and enthusiasm.

This rare ice storm, our first snow in seven years, made everything feel surreal. Houston, a city that thrives on sunshine and barbecue, seemed to have forgotten how to function in this icy grip. The biting cold stung my cheeks. With every step on the frozen parking lot, the crunch of ice underfoot mirrored the **anxiety** tightening around my heart.

Unexpected Setback

I woke up the next day at my mom's apartment, only to realize my **car was gone**. Was this a joke? Please, God, let this be a joke. Frantic calls to the police confirmed that my car had been **towed**. I stood there, seething with anger, the biting cold amplifying my sense of helplessness. Only in Houston would I lose my car to a tow truck during a snowstorm.

I paced the parking lot, the icy wind biting at my face, trying to piece together my next move. Instead of attending to my mom's needs at the hospital, I now had to retrieve my car. This unexpected task only added to my **vulnerability,** eroding what little confidence I had left. It felt as if life itself was mocking my attempts to manage everything.

Determined to figure things out **alone**, I resolved to retrieve my car without bothering anyone else. My **stubbornness** clung to me like a shadow, refusing to let me reach out for help, as if admitting defeat would shatter something fragile inside me.

At the tow yard, the attendant's words, "Reserved parking is for residents," felt like a cruel joke, reminding me how we can easily be overwhelmed by life's challenges and make mistakes.

It was a reminder that sometimes, the consequences we face are not **personal attacks** but simply the result of our actions. Paying the fine felt like rubbing salt on an **open wound,** each penny reminding me of my failures. I wondered how I could face the mounting challenges ahead.

Seeking Comfort

My autistic nephew looked at me, at a loss for words. He placed his hand on my head, trying to console me, perhaps pitying my short hair. His eyes spoke volumes without uttering a word. A lone tear trickled down my cheek, and I was reminded that some days, life is just hard. Some days are just rough. And some days, you **just have to cry** before you move forward. And all of that is okay.

The Power of Asking for Help

The day's challenges broke through my barrier of **isolation**, leaving me shattered and on the verge of **breaking down**. The overwhelming pain of dealing with my challenges eclipsed the **shame** of asking for help; it was simply too much to **bear alone.** As I dialed a friend for assistance, my hands trembled, numb from the cold—a small **surrender** to vulnerability.

My friend referred me to a nurse for help. Surprisingly, the nurse who answered was my neighbor, whom I'd never spoken to despite living next door for years. Her calm voice was a beacon, gently reminding me, "We all need each other in this world." Her words not only soothed my immediate panic but also marked a **turning point** in how I viewed seeking support.

Finding Connection

After seeking help, I found the **courage** to reach out to my colleagues at work. Within a few days, we started a short fundraiser with close friends to help with the hospital bills. I realized that help had been right next to me, but I had **built a wall** of shame around myself. One of the leaders at our organization even provided me with a contact at a nonprofit organization for additional support.

Inspired by this revelation, I began looking for ways to connect more with my local community. I discovered another local **non-profit group** that met regularly, its members united by a shared understanding and empathetic smiles, proving that no one has to face their **darkest** days in isolation. Joining this group became a crucial step in my journey. It allowed me to reach out to others and encourage them to seek help through the community check-ins program.

This ordeal taught me a profound lesson: seeking help is not a sign of weakness but a courageous step toward navigating life's icy challenges. We all need **each other,** but it's crucial to balance your time and energy.

Overcoming Hyper-Independence

Reflecting on this, I realized how many people, myself included, suffer from **hyper-independence,** often rooted in past **trauma.** Understanding how deeply rooted this behavior can be, I have firsthand experience with the challenges it presents. Research shows that even **young children** can feel this way, and many people worry about the pain of being rejected.

Hyper-independence often arises as a trauma response, developing when someone has faced neglect, **abuse,** or other traumatic experiences, leading them to rely solely on themselves for survival. While this **coping mechanism** may have been essential in the past, it can solidify into a rigid trait in adulthood, making it challenging to form deep personal and emotional connections.

If asking for help feels overwhelming, don't let **shame** or ego hold you back. Reach out—picture a community ready to lift you and support you through your darkest times. If you're in a place to help, be the reason someone feels welcome, seen, heard, valued, loved, and supported.

Final Reflection

Remember, you're not alone. In our darkest moments, we find our greatest **strength** in each other or unexpected strangers. Reflecting on this, I'm reminded of Lori Deschene's words: "You are not your struggles. You are the survivor who keeps moving forward despite them."

Are you suffering silently?

Midlife Crisis:
Finding Your Own Balance

The Escape

At 40, I decided to embark on a **midlife crisis** intervention plan. Avoiding my marital problems and skipping therapy, I turned to cycling. Each ride's exhilaration offered a brief escape from my emotional chaos.

Unable to get enough of the endorphins, I started cycling to work, covering more than 50 miles a day. This **obsession** led me to increasingly neglect my family responsibilities, opting for long bike rides over family time.

I would get home too tired to truly connect with my ex-wife and kids. I saw the hurt in their eyes, but the call of the open road was too strong. My ex-wife's face would light up with a hopeful smile when I walked in, only to dim as I slumped on the couch, **drained** and distant. My kids, eager to share their day, learned to approach me with

43

caution, their excitement tempered by my fatigue. My daughter, once so eager for my help with her homework, began to **avoid** asking for help after receiving bad grades, sensing my distraction more than my guidance.

As I pedaled through miles of the open road, I felt **free,** but the distance I put between myself and my family grew with each ride. Ironically, as I grew physically stronger, my relationships weakened. To mask my guilt and shame, I rode even more, creating a strange cycle of escape and **avoidance.** I pedaled harder, each mile a desperate attempt to leave it all behind, yet my shadow, my own relentless reflection, clung to me like a second skin, never letting me forget the weight of who I am.

I even tried listening to **gospel music** during my rides, hoping its messages of redemption and forgiveness would ease my conscience. Yet, the more I listened, the more I felt the weight of my actions, driving me to pedal harder and farther from home.

The Challenge

One sunny Saturday morning, I decided to push myself further and joined my old bike club teammates for a 90-mile loop. They were elite **Ironman competitors** with advanced gear. Excited yet apprehensive, I tried to latch onto their group. Their thrilling pace sharply contrasted with my relaxed rhythm. As my friends appeared fitter and stronger, I felt increasingly **slow and aged.**

Liam, the least serious cyclist, with his Texas tattoo on his arm, zoomed past me, yelling, "Come on, dude! Keep up!"

Jacky, with her rosebud mouth, glanced at me, her eyes a mix of excitement and humor. **"Show us what you've got!"**

Mark, the team leader, grinned. "Let's roll, bro."

Their camaraderie both encouraged and stung. They conversed easily at high speeds while I struggled to keep up.

The Ego

"I'll show them I'm not **old**," I quipped as my **ego** gnawed on me. Determined, I pushed myself to stay with the group, my legs aching and my heart pounding with every pedal stroke.

"Come on, Mr. Kenya, you're falling behind," another rider taunted.

Though well-meant, their supportive remarks felt **patronizing** and fueled my determination. The sting of their words and the burn of humiliation on my cheeks made me question myself. Their confident smirks and effortless strides only deepened my self-doubt. What was I trying to prove, and to whom was I trying it?

Approaching a wooden bridge, **fear** gripped me at the thought of slipping. My heart raced, and my grip tightened on the handlebars. Memories of past falls and injuries flashed through my mind, almost feeling the sting of gravel digging into my skin again. I slowed down, but it was too late. My front wheel wobbled uncontrollably, and in an instant, **I lost control**. I was flung into the air, and for a brief moment, time seemed to freeze. The world tilted, and I saw the sky, the bridge, and then the ground rushing up to meet me.

The Fall

The impact was excruciating. **Pain** shot through my side like a lightning bolt, and I lay there, gasping for breath, my body **screaming in agony.** Every attempt to move sent waves of pain crashing over me. As I tried to sit up, a Good Samaritan appeared, pointing and exclaiming in shock, "Your bone is sticking out!"

As I watched Liam and the group disappear into the horizon, my **isolation** felt palpable. I had pushed so hard to keep up, but for what? The realization that I needed to find my own rhythm hit me with the same force as the ground. I wanted to **blame** someone but realized my crisis was misguided by my own **selfish** midlife crisis plans.

The Aftermath

Luckily, another **Good Samaritan** drove me to the nearest emergency room. Just minutes earlier, I could ride my bike unassisted; now, I couldn't even put on my seatbelt. After multiple X-rays and hours of throbbing pain, I learned I had **broken four ribs** and shattered my **collarbone**. Anger flared within, a fiery rage directed at my own recklessness. Each jolt of pain was a bitter echo of the freedom I was about to lose.

As I lay in the **hospital bed** in pain, the fraudulence of that moment struck me. The throbbing in my collarbone was relentless, a physical manifestation of the **internal conflict** I had been avoiding.

Each pulse of pain was a reminder that the pace I had set was never truly mine. Even simple tasks, like bending over to **put on pants** with broken ribs, became nearly impossible. It felt like an Olympic event. For a brief, desperate moment, the thought of wearing my **ex-wife's dress** crossed my mind. Maybe she was onto something.

I realized I had been chasing a **facade of strength and youth**, pretending to be someone I wasn't. The irony was clear: trying to escape my problems, I created new challenges. I realized that all my efforts to avoid facing my issues had only led me to this painful reckoning. This wasn't just a physical injury—it was a wake-up call.

The Healing

After this incident, losing my bike unexpectedly turned out to be a positive change. Without it, I had nowhere to **hide** and was forced to face my own issues. They say wounds only heal when scabs fall off, and with my bike gone, I had to confront my **wounds** head-on. The rawness of my emotions—fear, anger, anxiety, and sadness—intertwined as I struggled with the reality of my situation.

For weeks, I grappled with these overwhelming feelings. It wasn't easy, but finally, I limped into **marriage counseling,** carrying both physical and emotional **scars**. I was determined to let my wounds heal, no matter how painful the process. This experience taught me to prioritize what's truly important in life. Just as I had to set my own pace in cycling, I realized I needed to set my own pace in life.

Reflecting on my journey, I ask you: Are you maintaining your own pace in life, or are you trying to keep up with the Joneses? Consider this: Would you make the same **decisions** without your friends influence?

How can you tell if you're trying to keep up with the Joneses? Pay attention to whether your decisions are **influenced** more by external validation or by your true desires. True growth comes from within, and each step on your terms leads to genuine fulfillment. What step can you take today to honor your own rhythm?

Consider these actions to break free from the cycle of comparison:

1. **Pause before You Act:** When making a decision, take a moment to reflect on whether it aligns with your personal values or if it's driven by a desire to match others.

2. **Do the Opposite of the Joneses:** Consider what the Joneses would do—then deliberately do the opposite. If everyone's splurging on the latest trend, try **embracing minimalism**. If everyone's rushing to follow a popular path, explore an unconventional one—like learning a niche skill or pursuing an unexpected passion. This

contrarian approach can help you break free from **societal pressures** and discover what truly resonates with you.

3. **Practice Gratitude:** Regularly remind yourself of what you have and why it matters to you. Gratitude can help shift your focus from what you lack to what you cherish.

Remember, it's **your journey.** Find balance and happiness by setting your own pace. Be **patient,** as good things take time. True fulfillment comes with each step taken on your terms.

Do Your Kids' Homework.
No One Is Coming To Save You.

The Silence of Loneliness

After my **divorce** in 2018, the silence of my new home was deafening. A stark contrast to the lively chaos of the past. Nights were the hardest. The absence of my children unleashed a tsunami of emotions. The dim glow of the TV and endless scrolling on social media only intensified my **solitude**. My bed became both a refuge and a battlefield—haunted by echoes of **past decisions.**

Can you remember a time when silence felt overwhelming? If you were faced with an overwhelming silence, how do you think you would cope with it?

Seeking Solace in Routine

Weekends with my **children** provided a brief respite. Laughter and shared stories temporarily lifted the veil of loneliness. During the days after work, I often delayed returning to my **"bed of thorns"** by visiting grocery stores, hoping to dilute the silence at home. The comforting aroma of fresh bread briefly lifted my spirits. But **being surrounded by strangers magnified my loneliness.** I even looked forward to telemarketers' calls, stretching the conversations for hours just to **escape** the solitude. Have you ever found comfort in unexpected places?

A Moment of Realization

One quiet evening, the silence was shattered by a call from my daughter about her forgotten homework. **"Dad, I need my homework,"** she said, her voice a lifeline in the quiet. As I fetched her homework, I came across a page with the words, **"What's going to make today special?"** Those words hit me like a punch to the gut, leaving me breathless and reeling. I stood there, frozen, overwhelmed by a mix of surprise and introspection. At that moment, **vulnerability** and determination collided with me.

Though miles away, it felt like my daughter was right there, challenging me to find **the answer**. The words felt like a challenge— one that demanded I step up, not just for her, but for myself. In the past, I had helped my daughter **fail** with her math homework, a failure that had haunted me ever since. But seeing those words now, I felt something shift inside me.

Have you ever had a moment when a **simple question** changed your perspective?

Facing Change Head-On

This question prompted me to ask, "What if?" daily. I taped the question by my bed, hoping my past struggles would gradually transform into blossoms of hope. It soon became clear: while we can lie to others, **lying to ourselves** is impossible. The words on my wall echoed this truth, seeping into the **heavy silence** I had tried to escape, filling every corner of my once lonely space. Like sunlight breaking through heavy clouds, they began turning the thorny underbrush of my doubts into a vibrant landscape of hope and **renewal.**

The Power of a Question

The question lingered in silence, its significance growing with every passing moment. "What if today could be special?" I couldn't shake the thought. Each realization nudged me to take action, quietly unlocking doors to new possibilities and gently healing **old scars**. With each step, new paths revealed themselves, propelling me forward and allowing past wounds to begin healing.

Think about it: What if today could be special for you? What small steps can you take to make it so?

Building a New Routine

Mornings dawned with doubt. But I pushed through. Facing the **"graveyard"** of my loneliness, I found resolve in a structured workout routine. Each day, I went for a short walk at nearby park—ironically, just a mile from an actual graveyard. As I passed the rows of tombstones, I couldn't help but wonder—had **the dead** ever faced moments like mine? On the hardest days, when I didn't feel like walking, I'd think, "I could be **six feet under** with no chance at this." And so, I kept going.

There were days I laid in bed, unable to muster an ounce of energy to move. Other days, I managed to rise, splash cold water on my face, and then retreat back to the sheets. I knew this was part of my healing journey, and it wasn't going to be easy. A life filled with small steps and stubborn persistence. Placing my walking shoes next to the door felt like a form of accountability. I added simple stretches, knowing they calm the body and boost serotonin, helping stabilize mood and reduce **depression.** This daily commitment steadied and strengthened me.

Despite the **temptation** to hit snooze or skip sessions, the routine became my anchor, bolstering my **resolve against fatigue** and temptation. During those workouts, I often found **clarity,** reflecting on my journey and the question by my bed. Each drop of sweat was a testament to my growing **strength** and resilience.

The words on my wall stood like a **tombstone,** a stark reminder: no one was coming to save me. I had to push through. From simple stretches to consistent daily workouts, my routine evolved into my lifeline. After a month, each new day brought clarity and a strengthened sense of self.

What **daily commitment** can anchor you and help build your resilience?

A Journey of Resilience

I learned that you can keep going long after you think you can't. If we are facing the right direction, all we have to do is keep on walking. My journey revealed life's zigzag path of hidden lessons, showing me that facing challenges with daily purpose can transform our outlook. Each morning, the question, "What's going to make today special?" taught me to navigate my days with **intention** and recognize the special in each day. I realized then that I'm a survivor, not a victim.

Your Transformative Question

If you're going through a rough patch in life, remember that everybody has a chapter they don't read out loud. Take a moment. Sit back. Marvel at your life. **The mistakes** that gave you wisdom, and the suffering that gave you strength. Despite everything, you still move forward. Be proud of the progress, no matter how small. Continue to endure, continue to persevere, and remember, no matter how dark it gets, the **sun will rise again.**

What part of your story can you marvel at today?

Witnessing the profound impact of a **simple question,** I now ask you: Are you ready to find your transformative question? Do you start your day with **purpose,** or do you just go through the motions? Embrace the challenge to make each day special by engaging with your own transformative question. **Write it down,** place it where you can see it daily, and let it guide your actions. What question will you ask yourself each day to inspire change?

May you find the strength to win the **loudest battles**—the ones you don't talk about.

"It takes a great man to be a good listener."
– Calvin Coolidge

Toilet Paper Trails:
Finding Wisdom in Embarrassment

Racing against Time

It was a typical evening in early 2021 when my routine took an unexpected turn. After work, I raced through a Houston park, heart pounding, the **clock ticking down**. This time, though, I was in a rush to make it to my daughter's dance class, where I had an important speaking role. With no time for a proper shower and desperate to beat rush hour, I skidded to a stop at a gas station, hastily wiping down and changing out of my **biking clothes.**

The restroom reeked of ammonia and mildew, making my eyes water and my throat tighten. Covering my nose with my shirt, I grabbed some toilet paper for a quick clean. I gagged on the foul air, my nose hurt, and I was ready to get out of there. Completely unaware of the comic relief I was about to provide, I hurried toward the exit.

The bathroom cleaner called out, "Sir!" I ignored him, dismissing his words as unimportant in my rush to reach the dance rehearsal. Have you ever **disregarded** someone because of their profession? I did that day, and soon regretted it.

Forgotten Detail

Upon arriving, sweaty and anxious, I took my place on stage, ready to impart wisdom to the attentive parents and eager dancers. As I began to speak, I felt a slight tug at the back of **my pants.** I dismissed it at first, chalking it up to nerves or maybe just my pants shifting with my movement.

I continued, forcing a smile, but a creeping **dread** swept over me. There it was again—a subtle pull that sent a jolt through me. I hesitated, discreetly reaching back, my fingers brushing the bare fabric of my pants. What could it be? I glanced around the room, taking in the sea of expectant faces, the soft rustle of programs in restless hands. My heart sank. Lord, I had **forgotten my underwear** in the bathroom. I was horrified. My cheeks burned with mortification as I imagined every eye in the room on me. I felt naked while fully dressed. Then a thought crossed my mind—maybe underwear can be overrated.

The Unraveling

Determined not to let it distract me, I pressed on. But then, I noticed the crowd's reaction shifting. Murmurs grew louder, and **stifled giggles** spread through the room. My mind raced. Oh no, how could they tell? I tried to ignore it, but the sound of amusement seemed to swell with each passing second. Beads of sweat trickled down my face, and I could feel my face flushing with **embarrassment.** The giggles turned into hushed chuckles, painting a clear picture of my predicament. I felt my throat tighten, each breath shallow and quick, as if my body was betraying me too.

My confusion quickly turned to terror as I realized, mid-speech, why the toilet cleaner was trying to get my attention. The trail of **toilet paper** I had unknowingly tucked into my pants at the gas station was now on full display. Frozen with leaden feet and a racing mind, I stood there in shock, wearing a plastic smile. Sweat spread under my arms as I teetered between laughing and crying. I was caught in a wave **shame and absurdity**. My heart pounded as I faced my negligence, now a comical spectacle under the glaring spotlight.

Lessons in Laughter

The laughter from the audience felt both **painful and humbling**. It was a stark reminder of my vulnerability and humanity. As the toilet paper unrolled behind me, so did my preconceptions. This moment of humility came when least expected but most needed. Ironically, it happened just after the **pandemic,** when memories of the toilet paper scarcity were still fresh. I sighed, relieved that they didn't know I had no underwear.

"Now we know who's been hiding all the toilet paper," I quipped, to the audience's amusement.

Finding Wisdom in Everyday Interactions

This **embarrassing** incident propelled me into deep reflection. It was not just about the laughter or the embarrassment but about the humility and connection these shared moments fostered. Every chuckle in the crowd reminded us of our shared human experiences and the unexpected wisdom they carry.

The **comical mishap,** marked by a strand of toilet paper, imparted a lesson on the nuances of human connections. It vividly illustrated how **wisdom** often eludes us when **we hurry** through our lives, too focused on our own concerns to notice the insights others might offer. Often, we're too quick or **biased**, missing learning opportunities. Wisdom can emerge from anywhere: a child's innocent remark, a neighbor's advice, or even the grocery man's tip on preserving avocados.

Since then, I've made a conscious effort to **pay more attention** to those around me. I listen intently when my church parking attendant shares his thoughts or when my children give input. This newfound openness has prevented further mishaps and enriched my life in surprising ways, revealing that lessons are often hidden in **obvious places.**

Remember, every interaction holds potential wisdom. At that moment, I wiped away my shame with the very strip of toilet paper trailing behind me, only to find that humility and **wisdom** had been tucked within it all along. For those in a rush or prejudice, there is always a **toilet paper moment** awaiting to happen—a reminder that ignoring someone can lead to an unexpected lesson in humility.

Take a moment now to think about the people you interact with daily. Next time you meet someone like a cashier, waiter, or security guard, **pay attention** to what they have to say. Often, those in seemingly humble roles are passed over, their words lost in the background noise of daily life. But there is a quiet strength in being overlooked—a resilience that builds when your existence is acknowledged only in fleeting moments.

Do you feel ignored because of your profession? If so, remember that your voice matters, and so do the voices of those around you. Sometimes, the most profound insights come from those who have learned to speak softly, to those who truly listen.

Reflect on the moments when **unexpected wisdom** passed you by. How have these experiences shaped who you are, and how will you **embrace** such insights in the future? As you ponder this, consider whether there are voices you dismiss because of the roles or jobs they occupy—might they hold the very **wisdom you seek?**

Life in Boots:
Navigating Storms and Relationships

Overgrown Surprises

Growing up in Kenya, my special rain boots were more than just childhood footwear; they symbolized the **personal journeys** we undertook to evolve and let go. I wore them during rainy seasons, and they supported my 10-mile walk to school. While I wore boots, some children walked barefoot, highlighting the disparities. Each pair of boots boosted my confidence.

Splashing through muddy puddles, I felt like a prized boxer entering a ring—ready to face watery challenges. These muddy treks represent our life's paths, where sometimes we **diverge** from others.

These boots protected my feet through life's literal and metaphorical storms. Even as I **outgrew them**, I found it hard to let go. I held onto those boots much like how we cling to outworn relationships out of fear. As my feet grew, the once-empowering boots began to **constrict,** echoing the struggles of evolving relationships. During dry seasons, they stayed under my bed like dormant friendships, hiding more than memories.

Lessons Learned

Life often presents **unforeseen challenges**. One stormy season, I hurried to retrieve cattle and hastily put on my boots. A strange sensation halted me—**a squirming,** slithering movement inside the boot. My heart raced as I kicked, **screamed**, and stomped my leg on the floor. After what felt like an eternity, a small **snake** finally slithered out, and I collapsed, both horrified and relieved.

Trembling with fear, I couldn't fathom putting my feet into those boots again. This terrifying encounter taught me a crucial lesson. Just as I had initially dismissed the odd feeling in my boot, we often ignore discomforts in our lives, hoping they will vanish. We overlook signs of **toxic relationships** or situations **constricting our growth**, only to be surprised when we find ourselves in desperate need and run for help. This experience forced me to recognize the importance of heeding these signals.

When was the last time you faced an unexpected challenge that made you adapt quickly?

Facing sudden fears, like a snake hidden in our boots, requires the same courage needed to **acknowledge** and address the need for change in our relationships. Moreover, this incident reinforced a vital lesson about growth: releasing the familiar is essential. It reflects the broader journey in personal relationships, where letting go is necessary to avoid stagnation and foster progress. Are you still holding on to stagnant friendships?

Practical Steps

Here are three clear signs that it might be time to **let go** of certain relationships:

1. Serious betrayal, which undermines trust.

2. Negative impact on your mental health.

3. One-sidedness, where you give much more than you receive.

Think about your current relationships. Do you see any of these signs? If so, it might be time to reevaluate. As Wesley Snipes said, "**Your circle** should want to see you win. Your circle should clap the loudest when you have good news. If they don't, get a new circle."

Just as I gave my **old boots** to my younger cousin, releasing outdated bonds can make space for new growth. As we outgrow old boots, we must also part with relationships that no longer serve our growth. Some options include telling the person directly that you are ending the friendship, allowing the friendship to fade away by communicating less over time, or discontinuing all communication immediately if someone is violating your **boundaries** or if you feel unsafe.

I once saw someone online advising that instead of deleting phone numbers of those you no longer wish to connect with, you can simply save them as "Don't answer 1." "Don't answer 2." "Definitely don't answer 3." And so on. It's a lighthearted but effective way to maintain your boundaries and protect your peace of mind.

Reflective Questions

Consider this past year: Have your relationships fostered your growth or **hindered** it? Letting go, though difficult, is essential for making room for relationships that support your true self and open doors to new beginnings. Stick with people who pull the magic out of

61

you, not the madness. **Celebrate** the progress of friends who move on to paths that better suit their stride. Understand that sometimes it's not personal—it's simply a matter of outgrowing what no longer fits. Embrace new individuals who can support your upcoming challenges, bringing fresh perspectives and energy into your life.

Conclusion

Reflect on the **"old boots"** in your life—habits, beliefs, or relationships that no longer serve you. Just as I had to **let go** of my worn-out boots, it's essential to release what holds you back. Change is not merely about finding new paths but transforming into your true self.

Are you ready to take the first step towards **your transformation?** Embrace change, release the old, and step into a future filled with growth and new opportunities. Your journey to a better self, starts now.

Summary:

Growth intertwines with emotional intelligence, relationships, and habits. This section explores how managing emotions fosters personal development, meaningful connections, and transformative habits. Together, these elements guide us toward a balanced, fulfilling life.

Part III:
Self-Discovery and
Personal Growth

Explore the depths of your true potential through the stories and lessons in this section. Illuminate your path to **personal development** with introspection, self-awareness, and continuous learning. Embrace the lifelong process of growth fueled by the courage to explore, the willingness to change, and the determination to become the best version of yourself.

> *"Sometimes it's wiser to let the storm pass*
> *than to challenge the thunder."*
> – Warren Buffett

Awakenings by Lake Naivasha: Respecting the Rhythms of Life

Drawn to Nature's Symphony

Before the pandemic, I was drawn to **Lake Naivasha** in Kenya's Great Rift Valley. More than just a scenic spot, it was a natural orchestra. The cacophony at first sounded like the rush of a waterfall. Only later did I discover it was the thousands of **flamingos** lining the shore, their calls blending with the rustling trees as if whispering secrets. The faint, rounded humps of **hippo snouts** breached the water's surface, reflecting the calm around them. The town's captivating tree line, hugging the lake's edge, held **a seductive charm.**

Serenity amidst the Vibrant Life

As I walked along the lake's edge to rent a boat, the lively chatter of **hawkers** selling artifacts mingled seamlessly with the tranquil environment. Amidst this vibrant yet peaceful setting, I felt a deep sense of calm. A white **dog** lay undisturbed in the middle of the footpath. Its presence reminded me of a lion lounging in the savannah. It appeared lifeless at first, but as I approached, I saw its chest gently rising and falling, **mirroring** the lake's tides.

The "bodaboda" taxi motorbikes rode just inches away from the dog, making me wonder if I should save it. I was in my saving-dog mode—perhaps I'd watched too many shows on The Dog Whisperer. Nearby, a rough-looking man, perhaps the **town's madman,** lay on the side of the road. I paid no attention and continued taking pictures, lost in the beauty of the lake.

A Moment of Tension

While attempting to snap a **selfie with the dog**, it twitched awake. Its sudden growling and bared teeth sent a chill down my spine. My heart pounded. The **dog rose**, muscles rippling under its fur, eyes locked on me, ready to lunge. **I was cornered.** Behind me was a **hippo-filled** lake and an aggressive dog in front of me. I clutched my phone as if it was my lifeline. The tension was suffocating, every second stretching into eternity under the gaze of the locals, some with their phones out, eager for a **viral moment.** Suddenly, I had become the spectacle of the town, the centerpiece of an unexpected drama that held everyone captive.

Desperation clawed at my thoughts. Should I **scream** for help or stay silent? My breath quickened, each inhale sharper than the last. Just as panic took hold, a piercing whistle—**"Wheewew!"**—cut through the tension. The dog froze, its snarl fading instantly. I felt a rush of relief as I turned to see the rough-looking man from earlier staring at me, his dagger eyes piercing my soul. His whistle had been the miraculous **interruption.** Disappointed sighs rippled through the onlookers, their anticipated drama cut short.

Reflecting on Calm and Restraint

Saved by a whistle. Clarity emerged as the dog begrudgingly settled back down and my adrenaline subsided. It reminded me of the importance of **restraint,** particularly when dealing with situations where our intervention might do more harm than good. A slap of reality. Just as I learned to step back and let the dog return to its rest, I began to see how, sometimes, offering **unsolicited help** or advice, especially to those resistant to change, can disrupt their journey. This calm after the storm, reflecting the lake's own serenity, taught me about the power of **silence** and thoughtful response. Chaos often teaches us the value of **"letting sleeping dogs lie,"** a lesson that resonates well beyond the immediate.

A Personal Anecdote of Financial Struggle

I thought about a friend of mine who faced financial difficulties yet clung to his love for **luxury cars**. Much like the tense moment with the dog, there were times when I felt the urge to step in, to force him to see reason. But I realized that, just as I couldn't force the dog to trust me, I couldn't force my friend to change his ways.

My experience by the lake reminded me that sometimes, stepping back and allowing others to **face the consequences** of their choices is the truest form of wisdom and compassion. Just as letting the dog lie was the right choice, so too was allowing my friend the space to navigate his own challenges.

Embracing the Wisdom of Restraint

It was then that I realized one of the greatest insights: not everyone is capable of immediate change, and accepting this can be a profound awakening. It's not ours to try to fix them. Sometimes, stepping back is necessary because continuous help can foster **dependency,** preventing personal growth. It can also be emotionally draining, impacting our well-being.

By always stepping in, we may unintentionally **enable negative behaviors**, hindering someone from facing their challenges independently. Establishing and respecting boundaries is crucial for healthy relationships, ensuring that our assistance does not infringe on personal space.

As Meredith Sapp wisely said, **"Mistakes are part of life.** Everyone makes them. Everyone regrets them. But some learn from them, and some end up making them again. It's up to you to decide if you'll use your mistakes to your advantage." Embracing this truth can be one of the most **powerful awakenings** we experience.

Reflecting on Personal Insights

Like the calm after my encounter with the dog, sometimes **stepping back** and letting events unfold on their own can lead to deeper insights. In your life, like the gentle rhythms of Lake Naivasha, how can patience and observation lead to wiser, more harmonious outcomes? In the stillness of reflection, true wisdom often emerges— quiet, profound, and enduring.

What are your own "sleeping dogs" that might benefit from restraint and reflection?

*You can find the **video** of the dog encounter on my social media channels (Wilhelm Mwengi) if you'd like to see more of this intense moment.*

"Your Emotions are the slaves to your thoughts, and you are the slave to your emotions."
– Elizabeth Gilbert

Ground yourself:
5-4-3-2-1 Discovery

The Weight of Responsibility

After my **mom's stroke** left her unable to care for herself, I became the sole caregiver for my autistic nephew, who lived with her. Although my ex-wife was taking care of our children, I felt less of a dad. The guilt of **neglecting my children** while moving in with my mother felt like a relentless tidal wave, overwhelming me.

Sleepless nights and loss of appetite made each day a battle. Happiness became an elusive dream, each moment tinged with **guilt.** It reached a point where being happy felt odd, so I avoided it. I found comfort in sadness. **I was happy being sad.** And the sadder I got, the better I felt. Yet, in my despair, I found a twisted comfort, sinking into a cold but familiar refuge. I didn't know then that these were signs of **depression.** I just thought it was my new normal.

Neglect and Isolation

Living on fast food drained my energy and dampened my enthusiasm for activities like biking. I felt stuck, torn between different worlds. My heart longed for the simple wisdom of my childhood village, far from the mega-city where dreams seemed out of reach. Left with the emotional turmoil of supporting my mother and nephew, **I withdrew**. My friends often tried to fix the **chaos** around me, leaving the real chaos within me untouched.

I had previously asked for help when my mom was hospitalized, but now I didn't want to **bother anyone**. I felt this was my problem to figure out alone. I avoided asking for help because I didn't want to seem entitled, selfish, or bothersome—a behavior I later learned is called "**over-empathizing** with others."

Finding Grounding through the 5-4-3-2-1 Technique

One rainy day, a friend dragged me **to volunteer at a church**, promising food. I went, hoping to find other miserable souls; misery loves company, after all. The event was noisy, and **my mood worsened** with the rain. Amidst the rain's murmur against the church windows, a community leader stepped up to the microphone.

"We're going to try something called the 5-4-3-2-1 technique," she said, her voice calm and reassuring.

I crossed my arms skeptically, leaning towards my friend. "Really? We came here for this?" I whispered.

"It's worth a shot," my friend replied, patting my shoulder. "Just listen."

Experiencing the Technique

The leader continued, "This technique helps **ground you by** focusing on your senses. Start by noticing five things you can **see** around you..."

I sighed but decided to follow along. "Alright, let's see what this is about," I thought, scanning the room.

"...four things you can feel and **touch**," she continued.

I ran my fingers over the rough fabric of the chair. It felt grounding strangely.

"...three things you can **hear**."

I closed my eyes, tuning into the hum of the air conditioning and the distant chatter of volunteers.

"...two things you can **smell**," the leader's voice softened.

The faint scent of perfumes wafted through the room, mingling with the smell of rain-soaked earth.

"...and one thing you can **taste**."

I noticed the lingering taste of my breakfast, a reminder I needed to see a dentist. To my surprise, I felt a **subtle shift**, a quieting of the chaos in my mind.

Finding Hope and Calm

That evening, despite the neighbors' kids thumping above, I was determined to try again. Was I grasping at straws? Maybe. But I needed something to hope for. I kept at it, repeating the 5-4-3-2-1 technique over and over. At first, the overwhelming noise around me seemed **impossible to ignore,** but with each attempt, the chaos began to blur. Slowly, the sounds faded, inch by inch, until a sense of calm started to settle in. It wasn't instant, nor was it easy. But **gradually**, with practice, I found myself closer to peace than I had been in a long time.

Sharing the Technique and Its Benefits

I shared the technique with my mom, though at first, she was **resistant** and skeptical. It seemed too simple to be effective, and she doubted it could help with the frustration of losing her voice and ability to eat. But over time, it became her daily ritual, helping her cope with the challenge.

On particularly frustrating days, her anger came through in abrupt text messages. Losing her voice was a constant struggle, and sometimes even the wrong gum flavor would set off a wave of frustration, as she needed the gum to keep her mouth muscles functioning.

In those moments, when frustration peaked, I would lock myself in my car, seeking a few minutes of **solitude** to practice the **technique**. My nonverbal nephew would observe me keenly and join in, thinking it was a game. This shared ritual brought us both calm, helping me stay composed and gather the strength needed to support her through those difficult moments.

Gradually, as I continued practicing, the benefits became noticeable. The **mental fog** began to clear, and my overthinking started to fade. The 5-4-3-2-1 technique disrupts **negative thought** patterns by anchoring your focus to the present moment—redirecting your attention to physical sensations, effectively breaking the loop of overwhelming thoughts.

My sleep improved; I started waking up **refreshed,** no longer dreading the day ahead. The **anxiety** that once kept me awake until morning began to dissipate, and I no longer felt like a **walking zombie,** stumbling through my days in a haze. Instead, my focus sharpened, allowing me to tackle tasks with a clarity I hadn't experienced in years.

When I received those texts laced with anger, this was my go-to method for regaining **composure.** Each morning, before walking into the office, I would pause in my car and practice this technique. On my way home, I did the same, reinforcing the newfound sense of calm and focus that had become a part of my daily routine.

This **simple ritual** grounded me, providing a much-needed respite from the chaos of daily life. As days passed, even the morning sunlight grew brighter. The neighborhood's chatter transformed into a melodious backdrop to my renewed focus. Sharing the technique with others amplified its value. Whether with **volunteers, students, or friends**, each shared moment reinforced its effectiveness. On weekends, when I saw my kids, it became a cherished part of our time together. We would all take a moment to ground ourselves, finding peace amidst our busy lives.

A Beacon of Peace

If you feel **overwhelmed**, let this simple technique be your beacon. It's a light in the darkness, showing that peace comes from within. Take a brief pause, wherever you are, and notice:

Five things you can **see.**

Four things you can **feel** and touch.

Three things you can **hear.**

Two things you can **smell**.

One thing you can **taste**.

It's a **simple start**, but it's the first step toward reclaiming your calm. By engaging your senses, you ground yourself in the present, distancing from anxious thoughts about the past or future. This focused awareness helps you become more attuned to your thoughts and feelings, making them easier to manage effectively. Each mindful moment is a step toward serenity—a journey of not just coping but thriving amidst life's storms.

Remember, **simplicity attracts wisdom**. Take a deep breath, clear your mind, and listen—your heart is trying to tell you something.

> *"Pruning is a necessary part of life. To grow, we must give up the branches of ourselves that no longer serve us."*
> -Jessica Raymond

Pruning Life's Trees: Lessons from My Front Yard

New Beginnings

In the mid-2000s, in some **US suburbs**, especially in Texas, I noticed a peculiar pattern. Builders cleared the land of trees to lay **foundations** only to plant new ones once the homes were built. Typically, one tree for a 3 to 4-bedroom house and two for anything larger. This **re-planting** felt symbolic: a fresh start with each new home, a reminder that sometimes, to grow, we must first **let go.**

The Cost of a Front Yard Tree

After moving into our **new home**, we proudly noted we had a tree out front. Wow! I owned a tree in Texas. It felt like a major step, akin to owning a **camel or donkey** back home. I even wanted to baptize and name it. Having been raised in Kenya, where trees grew wild and free, I was oblivious to **"tree care."** Back home, trees were just... there, nurtured by God's free rain and sun. I felt a mix of **pride and disbelief** at the responsibility of caring for a single tree.

The next surprise? **Grass.** Equally shocking? I had to buy grass. Grass that served no purpose, just to sit there and look pretty—not even to feed livestock. **Absurd.** It felt almost like paying for air to breathe. Back home, the grass was wild and free. It carpeted the earth; no human effort was required.

I was ready to raise kids, not battle lawn and tree expenses. As if buying grass wasn't enough, I couldn't even raise chickens or a goat in my backyard. Nature was no longer mine to cultivate. Was anything here ever going to feel like home?

I found myself longing for the simplicity and freedom of my **homeland**—the way life felt more in tune with nature, less bound by rules and purchases. The sight of bare, brown patches in my backyard only deepened the contrast. The wild, untamed beauty of Kenya seemed like a distant dream, and the **weight of that loss** settled heavily on me.

Have you ever bought something valuable only to realize you were not ready for its **maintenance**?

The Importance of Pruning

One day, as I was wrestling with these thoughts, I saw my neighbor meticulously pruning his tree. His dedication puzzled me. I watched him carefully trim away the branches, wondering if that's what I'm supposed to be doing. At first, I shrugged it off, thinking he was either bored or an overzealous environmentalist. But within months, our tree was leaning like the Tower of Pisa, its **roots** threatening our home's foundation. This wake-up call made it clear that if you don't **prune**, your roots might grow outwards, risking stunted growth.

A Metaphor for Life

Instead of growing strong and wide, our tree branches started to droop down, becoming weaker and **less vibrant.** The Housing Authority duly dropped a notice: "Fix your tree!" Initially, I was angry and filled with **contempt**.

"Who are they to tell me what to do with my property?"

My **pride** was stung by the reprimand. Yet, as the initial wave of pride subsided, I saw this as a mirror to other aspects of my life. It wasn't just about the tree; it was a **reflection** of how I often **resisted** acknowledging areas that needed pruning.

Lessons Learned from Neglect

Seeing my neglected tree, I realized that **neglect** has its consequences, mirroring other areas in my life that need **attention**. The Housing Authority's notice served as a strong reminder that **external pressures** sometimes require internal reflection and change. For instance, if you let bad financial habits go unchecked, they can spiral out of control, just like **untamed roots.**

External Pressures, Internal Changes

With proper pruning and some stern pep talks, my tree transformed. Day by day, it grew stronger, its branches reaching out with newfound confidence. It stood tall and robust, drastically **enhancing** our home's curb appeal. To my surprise, it even started producing flowers I never knew it could grow. I watched in awe, each new bloom filling me with a profound sense of pride and **accomplishment**.

My neighbor once commented, "Good looking tree." I responded with a smile, feeling a deep connection to its journey, "I know," I said, standing there with quite pride. For a moment, I thought about hugging it, whispering words of encouragement to its sturdy trunk. "Look at you, **beautiful tree.**" I murmured, as if it could hear the admiration in my voice.

Transforming Through Care

Witnessing our once feeble tree now thriving, I saw parallels with my life. This experience taught me that the same care revitalizing our tree could **breathe life** into my neglected areas. I was anxious and impatient to see the tree **transform**, but the process taught me patience and perseverance.

Personal Growth and Reflection

Embracing this insight, I started identifying parts of my life that needed "pruning." My **unchecked spending** on cycling gear was the first to go. By cutting down on these expenses, I could invest in what genuinely **enriched my life,** like paying for piano lessons for my daughter. I replaced TV time with reading, allowing me to dive into new worlds and ideas. Reducing excessive long calls with friends helped me **focus** on caring for my expensive grass. Each of these changes allowed light to reach new buds of growth in my life. With that in mind, here are **three steps to help** you prune your life effectively

1. **Identify and Prioritize**: Take time to examine your habits. Ask yourself when the behavior usually occurs, who you're with, what happens, how you feel, and what **"payoff"** you get from it. This will help you identify the habits that are truly detrimental and prioritize which ones need immediate attention.

2. **Create and Implement a Plan**: Once you've identified the habits that need pruning, create a clear and actionable plan to address them. This could involve setting specific goals,

creating a schedule, or seeking support from trusted friends or professionals. For example, if you want to reduce TV time, set a limit on daily screen time and replace it with activities that **promote growth**, like reading or a new hobby.

3. **Embrace the Unconventional:** Sometimes, the most effective changes come from unexpected places. Consider unconventional methods like taking a **"digital detox"** weekend where you completely disconnect from all electronic devices. This break can give you a fresh perspective and help you reset your priorities. Another unconventional approach could be practicing "random acts of kindness," which can shift your focus outward and improve your overall sense of well-being.

Conclusion

Pruning isn't just about cutting back; it's about encouraging new growth. Recognize that each pruning cut, though sometimes painful, is a step towards a more **vibrant** and fulfilling life. Less pruning. Weaker roots.

When was the last time you examined your habits? What "tree" in your life needs attention? Maybe it's time to start pruning and allow new **growth** to flourish.

"When the archetypal image of what it means to be masculine becomes harmful and aspirational."

Toxic Masculinity:
From Condoms to Courage

High School in Kenya

In my Kenyan high school, when the government first introduced **condoms** through sponsored **"Family Planning"** clinics, an expired condom in your pocket—often crumpled and stolen from older boys—oddly became a badge of manhood. It was a confusing time when manhood was measured by odd tokens rather than genuine maturity.

Salt-N-Pepa's **"Let's Talk About Sex"** blared on every radio station, and we boasted about imaginary girlfriends to mimic a macho culture. We paraded our **counterfeit** symbols of manhood, but beneath the surface, we were just boys grappling with the daunting expectations of growing up in a rapidly changing world. I felt a mix of pressure and bewilderment, caught between wanting to **fit in** and questioning the absurdity of it all.

Condoms were hidden like the ugliness of the night—**shameful secrets** rather than symbols of responsible behavior. Traditionally, grandparents were the keepers of **secrets,** but when it came to matters like these, their wisdom had expired just like the condoms in our pockets. I remember my little cousins in the village proudly showing us their new balloons, not realizing they were condoms. I watched my aunt try to explain it to them, trying to bridge the gap between **innocence and reality.**

Those expired condoms symbolized the outdated beliefs about manhood we all secretly carried. We were all fumbling through the darkness, clutching at symbols that meant nothing, both clueless and searching for answers.

Persisting Beliefs

Four years in a boys-only boarding school **fueled by testosterone** reinforced these toxic ideas. In the dorms, our conversations revolved around proving our **"manhood"** through exaggerated tales of conquests and bravado. Challenging these notions was met with ridicule. The rigid hallways echoed with the unspoken rule: emotions were for the **weak.**

Our experience wasn't isolated; it reflected **deeper societal issues** tied to outdated notions of masculinity. Even after high school, these beliefs followed me, highlighting how deeply ingrained cultural norms persist beyond our initial environments. In our world, you either married or stayed single; dating was as foreign as the TV dramas we watched.

Cultural Expectations

When my mother found a condom in my pocket and demanded to know its origin, I felt a surge of **panic and shame.** Silence hang between us. Her disappointment cut deep, and at that moment, I realized just how much cultural expectations dictated our lives. This incident was a stark reminder of how **societal pressures** enforce outdated gender roles.

I came to understand toxic masculinity as a form of manhood rooted in the **suppression** of emotional expression and the avoidance of emotional management. Pain disguised as strength. Like many men, I felt **pressured** to trade my mental health for stereotypically masculine traits, suppressing emotions, refusing help, and resorting to aggression.

New Perspectives

Moving to the United States introduced me to new **perspectives** on masculinity. With American roommates, I saw condoms openly displayed in our apartment, a stark contrast to my previous life. They had different flavors, like candy in a store. **Freedom** and confusion collided. The **culture shock** forced me to reevaluate my understanding of manhood, exposing me to diverse perspectives and value systems. This exposure was crucial in **reshaping** my view of masculinity and understanding its impact on my life and mental health.

Unfortunately, the struggle to reconcile **conflicting cultural** expectations has led to tragic outcomes for some immigrant men in the U.S. Silent battles fought alone. Cases of **suicide** among this group have highlighted the devastating impact of isolation, unaddressed mental health issues, and the pressure to conform to rigid notions of masculinity. Change begins in the shadows.

Embracing Vulnerability

These experiences taught me that reaching out and **expressing vulnerability** is not just an act of courage but a profound strength. As Brené Brown said, "Vulnerability is not winning or losing; it's having the **courage** to show up and be seen when we have no control over the outcome." This profound truth guided my journey toward a healthier expression of manhood.

Personal Growth

To combat toxic masculinity, I had to break the **stigmas** in my own life. I sought opportunities for personal growth, such as attending a men's ministry at a local church and openly discussing men's issues without **judgment.** I was shocked to see a **man cry** from emotions that weren't caused by death. Vulnerability became strength. It was a moment that challenged my deeply ingrained beliefs about masculinity.

These experiences underscored the need for **broader societal** transformation. I realized that personal change could spark wider societal shifts, and that tackling toxic masculinity requires both personal and **collective efforts.** By challenging these norms personally, I began to see the potential for societal change.

Below are some ways we can help prevent toxic masculinity:

1. **Changing the Curriculum**: Including topics in school curricula about unhealthy relationships, safe social media, and the consequences of **violence**. For instance, introducing programs that teach empathy and emotional intelligence can foster healthier relationships.

2. **Educating Parents:** Teach parents about the importance of creating safe and nurturing environments and how physical punishment and **humiliation** can harm children. Workshops and seminars can equip parents with positive parenting techniques.

3. **Leading by Example:** Be inclusive, supportive, and healthy in your leadership. Leaders who model respectful and empathetic behavior set a powerful example for others to follow.

4. **Intervening**: Respectfully stop toxic masculinity when you see it, such as aggression, sexism, or oppression. Speaking up and challenging harmful behaviors in real time can make a significant impact.

Call to Action

My story underscores the urgent need to address toxic masculinity and take action. We must educate, empower, and share resources on healthy masculinity. Host community screenings on gender norms to spark valuable dialogues. Together, we can redefine manhood and **create supportive,** nurturing communities.

Conclusion

Let's take this opportunity to foster **healthier expressions of masculinity** and support each other in this transformative journey. By challenging outdated norms and embracing vulnerability, we can pave the way for a more **inclusive** and emotionally healthy society. Will you play your part?

Not Yet:
Unlocking Your Growth Potential

Navigating the First Steps of Success

In the fresh spring of the 2000s, I started at a **prestigious law firm** in Houston. Overwhelmed from the start, I felt like a young flower facing an unexpected frost. The constant clicking of heels and hushed discussions deepened my **isolation**, making "Excuse me" my frequent refrain as I navigated this daunting new world. I was beginning to taste the milk and honey of success, but my journey soon **hit a snag.**

Facing Early Challenges

I had just been promoted to computer technician, and one crushing afternoon, I found myself in a **desperate** battle with a stubborn photocopier. The promotion had felt like a small victory, a step closer to the success I craved, but this machine seemed determined to **test me**. It was the main copy source for critical print jobs needed for an important, high-profile case our firm was supporting. My hands trembled, and tears blurred my vision as frustration and **self-doubt** mounted. Every malfunction felt like a personal failure, and the weight of the firm's **expectations pressed** down on me, amplifying my anxiety.

The stakes were incredibly high, and the **pressure** was suffocating. The office buzzed with tension, mirroring my silent struggle. I reminded myself to **be brave** enough to be bad at something new, like young plants pushing through the soil, reaching for the promise of spring.

In that reflective moment, Imani, a warm-hearted legal assistant from Louisiana whom I had helped with computer problems before, approached with her southern accent,

"Mwengi, why are you fighting with that thing?" She chuckled warmly, adding, "Booy, you or that machine gonna have to win."

Her eyes softened with understanding, "Now, remember it's okay to feel overwhelmed," she murmured.

A Turning Point

When I confessed my fears, she met my gaze with unwavering compassion and said, **"Not yet."**

I looked at her, puzzled. "What do you mean?" I asked, my mind racing. Was she speaking in some Creole dialect I din't understand?

She smiled and continued, "Not yet, but I'm sure you will figure it out."

Her simple yet powerful words, **"Not yet,"** ignited a flicker of hope within me, shifting my **perspective** from defeat to possibility. As Aristotle said, "Patience is bitter, but its fruit is sweet." This reminds us that enduring the challenges of **learning** and growth ultimately leads to rewarding outcomes. While I didn't figure it out on my own that day, another copier was found to keep things running smoothly. But I knew, deep down, that my moment of **triumph** was just around the corner.

Lessons from Adversity

"Figure it out, Village boy," Creighton, the lead technician, sneered as he handed me another cryptic note. His words stung—a harsh reminder that I was still seen as an **outsider, unworthy** of **respect** in his eyes. Creighton was always rubbing shoulders with the executives, a constant reminder of his **influence** and status within the firm.

Back in the technician's room, I couldn't shake the feeling that he was deliberately trying to block my progress. He turned our interactions into a twisted scavenger hunt with obscure references, leaving me frustrated and determined to prove myself. Each encounter with Creighton felt like a battle. The only **weapons** I had were patience and **persistence.**

Each vague instruction felt like a deliberate attempt to sabotage my progress. He felt threatened by my presence as if I was going to snatch his job from him. Tension simmered between us, **a silent war** of wills. His dismissive smirk and condescending comments only fueled my determination. I would not let him undermine me.

He often shrugged off my questions or misplaced essential tools, leaving me to scramble **under pressure**. While I wasn't the most technical in our group, I excelled at calming stressed employees with computer issues, making me a **valuable partner** for tricky assignments.

One hectic day, as the clock ticked relentlessly, I asked him about the spare cables.

"Figure it out yourself," he muttered with a smirk.

My frustration spiked. I closed my eyes and said under my breath, "Not yet." I wasn't ready to give in. "**Not yet. I got this.**" Instead of backing down, the frustration only sharpened my resolve.

These high-stress situations became my proving ground. Each challenge felt like a riddle, pushing me towards "Not yet." Slowly, I learned that trusting myself was key. I began to see rejection not as a dead end but as a **redirection**. Every "no" nudged me towards self-reliance. The more he tried to **undermine me,** the more I realized my own strength. His challenges taught me that "most of the time, the person you need the most will teach you not to need anyone."

Embracing the "Not Yet" Philosophy

As the "not yet" philosophy spread among my coworkers, it transformed our approach to challenges. What once felt like impossible tasks, shrouded in anxiety and **fear of failure,** gradually began to look like puzzles waiting to be solved. Tasks that once seemed insurmountable, like mastering the photocopier or new software, became **opportunities** for growth.

During a particularly busy afternoon, I saw Mark, one of our new technicians, wrestling with the new inventory software. His frustration was palpable, a mirror of my own early struggles.

He looked up in exasperation, and I simply said, "Not yet, Mark. You'll get it."

He sighed, then smiled and went back to it with renewed determination. In that moment, I realized the power of the "not yet"

mindset was spreading, slowly replacing doubt with resilience. One day, Imani confessed with a smile,

"I read about the power of "yet" in a newspaper. It just popped into my head when I saw you."

Her **humble admission** made the philosophy even more meaningful to us. Never underestimate the power of planting a seed.

This revelation was cemented when I encountered **Carol Dweck's research** on the "power of yet." Dweck, a renowned psychologist, introduced the concept of a "growth mindset"—the belief that abilities and intelligence can be developed through effort and perseverance. In her studies, she found that students **praised** for their effort rather than their innate ability were more likely to embrace challenges and persist in the face of setbacks.

This scientific validation was powerful. It reinforced my own experiences and solidified the importance of the "Not Yet" philosophy. It fostered resilience, a willingness to learn, and a growth-oriented approach to life and work.

Daily Practice of "Not Yet"

Now, "not yet" is my **life mantra.** Each morning, as the sun casts shadows through my bedroom window, I challenge myself with something I've been avoiding, asking myself,

"What am I putting off because I don't feel ready?"

When faced with difficult learning challenges, like mastering a new skill or tackling a complex subject, remind yourself that you're not late. **You're on time.** The process was preparation. Your journey doesn't have to look like anyone else's and often will not match the timeline you created.

Embrace less shame and judgment and more compassion and **acceptance.** Let these words serve as a daily reminder that **your path is unique** and valuable and that your **growth** unfolds at its own pace.

Your "Not Yet" Journey Begins

With "not yet" as my guide, every hesitation becomes a prelude to action and every **setback** an opportunity for a comeback. This philosophy has reshaped my life, proving that "not yet" is not just for immediate challenges but a lifelong approach to growth.

Remember, this road may not have led you to where you want to be, but it will definitely lead you to where you're supposed to be. Embrace the "not yet" mantra in your own life. Identify a **daunting goal,** remind yourself it's not a matter of "if" but "not yet," and take those incremental steps forward.

Recently, Imani called me up. "So," she asked, her voice warm with curiosity, "have you published that book yet?"

Her enduring belief in the "not yet" philosophy continues to inspire me. And just like she encouraged me, I want to **pass that inspiration on to you.**

What's your "not yet?"

Procrastination:
A Twisted Tale in San Diego

The Perfect Trip

On a business trip to San Diego for a work-related conference, I experienced something **unforgettable** right before my flight home the next day. While dining by the marina with conference attendees, the breathtaking view stole our breath, and the rhythmic crashing of waves hinted at the **drama** about to unfold.

The Enemy of Procrastination

I had a bad habit of procrastinating. As a professional procrastinator, I always felt handcuffed by my **own delays,** which is how I ended up with a black Impala Sedan as my last-minute rental. Self-sabotage. Because I waited so long to book, it was the only available sedan within my price point—a decision made for me by my delay. It wasn't just a car; it was a reminder of every opportunity I'd let slip through my fingers.

Unbeknownst to me, this **simple choice** would teach me a profound lesson about the consequences of minor decisions. Have you ever made a trivial choice that dramatically altered your path?

The Unfolding Crisis

After lunch, I noticed my unlocked rental car—an unusual oversight—signaling the start of a **chain of events.** A gust of wind slammed the car door shut, setting off the alarm. The piercing sound drew curious glances from passersby. Sliding into the driver's seat, I turned the key—nothing. **Frustration** Surged. My anxiety mounted with each futile attempt, my grip tightening on the steering wheel, my knuckles turning red. In the back of my mind, a **nagging unease** started to creep in, a feeling that something wasn't right.

Why did I always wait until the **last minute**? My heart pounded, each beat echoing the urgency of my impending flight. I should have been more careful. Why didn't I double-check the locks? Suddenly, my phone vibrated with an urgent work call.

"Come on, not now," I muttered, feeling a surge of helplessness engulf me. The anxiety I felt earlier was morphing into **something darker,** a growing sense of dread. If only I had handled things earlier, I wouldn't be in this mess.

The Confrontation

Just as I reached for my phone, a shadow fell over the window, and my stomach clenched.

"Hands on the steering wheel, where I can see them!" a **police** officer appeared beside me, his gun ominously close.

My breath caught in my throat. Adrenaline surged. I froze. The dark muzzle of a **gun** inches away made my stomach churn with fear. My brain refused to process the sheer terror of the situation. As I gazed into the hollow of the gun's muzzle, my phone clattered to the dashboard, silenced mid-ring by the officer's stern gaze.

"Oh my God, this can't be happening," I thought, my mind racing.

"Show me your hands!" he repeated, his voice louder and more menacing.

"Get out of the car slowly," he ordered, then proceeded to **handcuff** me. My legs trembled uncontrollably, threatening to buckle beneath me.

"Officer, there's been a mistake," I said, trying to keep my voice steady. "This is a rental car. I can show you the paperwork. It's just... in my bag. In the trunk."

The officer's eyes narrowed. A woman hurried over, clutching her hand bad, her expression a mix of frustration and anger.

"Not today!" she yelled, pointing at me. "**I hope you rot in jail.**"

I could feel my chest tighten and my vision blur as dread flooded through me. How could this situation have spiraled so quickly? Especially here in beautiful San Diego, of all places? I noticed some of the conference attendees standing nearby, their faces shocked. Their presence made the **humiliation and fear** even more intense. They were probably thinking they'd had lunch with a **car thief.**

Time seemed to stretch painfully as he patted me down, found my wallet, and pulled out my ID. His stern expression softened slightly as he examined it, but his eyes remained hard.

"Let me see your car keys," he said.

I nodded towards the car, feeling a knot of **anxiety** tightening in my stomach.

"They're in the ignition," I said, my voice barely steady.

He shot me a wary glance before retrieving the keys and pressing the alarm button. The sound of the honk echoed down the empty street, loud and sharp. I felt immense solace. How had I not thought of that? I breathed a sigh of **relief** as I saw the lights of another black Impala flashing a block away. **Liberation**.

"Thank you, Lord," I whispered, my breath releasing a shaky sigh.

"Is that your car?" he asked, his eyes narrowing with skepticism.

He drove me to the identical car down the street. I retrieved the rental papers from the trunk, my hands trembling. He scrutinized them, matching the details with my ID. Finally, his posture relaxed.

"Alright, it checks out. Be careful next time; it could end much worse." His tone was stern but carried a hint of relief. I nodded, feeling the last remnants of tension drain away.

Reflection and Realization

As the **handcuffs** clicked open, I felt a wave of peace. It wasn't just the resolution of a misunderstanding; it was also a newfound awareness of my vulnerabilities and **assumptions**. I stood there—heart still pounding, relieved yet shaken. The air felt lighter, yet the real magnitude of the moment sank in deeply. I wondered how such a minor oversight had **escalated** so quickly. Could my procrastination have caused this spiral? This question reshaped my view of minor decisions as I replayed each step that led to this crisis.

This ordeal caused me to miss my flight. Standing at the airline counter with soiled pants, ready to make a rushed decision, I paused. This time, I took a deliberate pause to reflect. There was no time to procrastinate after this lesson. As I stood there, the **urgency** of the ticking clock urged me to think quickly but carefully.

Practical Steps and Moving Forward

I asked the agents detailed questions to separate useful facts from mere opinions and carefully considered the pros and cons of each flight option. **My goal** was clear—find a safe and timely way back home, allowing for calm after the storm. **Trusting my gut**, I selected the flight that promised not just a return but a chance to decompress.

Since then, each decision, no matter how small, has prompted careful thought. This incident has shaped my approach to life and work, infusing patience and foresight into my daily interactions.

I've come to appreciate the small victories in my day-to-day life, whether it's accomplishing everything on my **to-do list** or simply showing up. As Veronica Dearly wisely said, "Some days you feel good because you absolutely smashed everything on your to-do list. Other days, you feel good because you managed to take a shower. Whichever it is, I hope you find something that makes you feel good today."

To combat procrastination, here are four practical steps I've implemented:

1. **Use the Two-Minute Rule:** If a task will take less than two minutes to complete, do it **immediately.** This prevents small tasks from piling up and becoming overwhelming.

2. **Create a Distraction-Free Environment**: Set up a dedicated workspace free from distractions. This helps maintain focus and reduces the temptation to procrastinate.

3. **Accountability Partner**: Find someone who can hold you accountable for your goals and deadlines. **Regular check-ins** can motivate you to stay on track.

Weird Advice: Reward Yourself with Deliberate Procrastination

One unconventional tip that worked wonders for me is to schedule **deliberate procrastination**. Yes, you heard that right. By setting aside specific time slots where I allow myself to indulge in non-productive activities—like watching a favorite TV show or browsing social media guilt-free—I found it easier to focus during work times. Knowing I have a **dedicated procrastination** period reduces the urge to **slack** off during critical tasks. This **strange trick** turned my procrastination into a reward, making me more productive overall.

Final Thoughts

There are days when my mind fights to return to procrastination, especially when I'm doing something that's not fun, like working on Excel projects. But I've learned to give myself grace and get back to my good habits. Each decision not only brings **immediate consequences** but also sets the stage for unforeseen challenges and opportunities. Don't let procrastination handcuff you because a good plan today is better than a perfect plan tomorrow.

Take a moment. Decide. See how deliberate choices shape your path. Consider what tasks you are postponing, and avoid being a prisoner of your own delays. Remember, do it now. Sometimes, "later" becomes "never".

Summary:

Embarking on self-discovery reveals our true selves and potential. This section's stories highlight introspection, self-awareness, and continuous learning. Personal growth is a lifelong process fueled by courage, willingness to change, and determination to become our best selves.

Part IV:
Recognizing and Seizing Opportunities

Life is filled with hidden chances, often overlooked but full of potential. This section reveals how to spot and seize these moments through engaging stories and practical lessons. Learn to identify genuine opportunities, avoid **manipulative traps**, and discover the blend of bravery, innovation, and discernment needed for success. Be inspired to stay alert, make decisive moves, and build a life marked by achievement and integrity.

"A resourceful person will always make an opportunity fit his or her needs."
–Napoleon Hill

Resourceful Nights at Coco Loco: Lessons in Ingenuity

Discovering "Coco Loco"

During my college years in the early 2000s, I lived close to **"Coco Loco,"** a popular nightclub located on the southwest side of Houston. It was our **slice of Africa** in the US, blasting reggae and African tunes, complemented by a free Mexican buffet every Friday. However, its sketchy neighborhood made parking a gamble. As students on a **budget,** valet parking was out of the question. We opted for a spot a few blocks away, humorously dubbed "no man's land."

Meeting Rashon

In the shadowy corners of **"no man's land,"** we met Rashon, a **homeless** man battling the biting cold each night. He treated his patch of asphalt as more than a makeshift job—it was his steadfast claim to dignity and order in a life frayed at the edges. Stocky and scarred, with worn shoes and rough hands like the bark of an ancient oak, he carried the marks of battles fought in his past. Unyielding. He reminded me of the quiet, wise village men back home, whose eyes held the secrets of the mountains and whose words carried the weight of **forgotten legends.**

Rashon's Resilience

Despite his **circumstances**, Rashon carried a **dignity** that commanded respect. He watched over our cars for a modest fee, becoming our affordable valet and an unexpected confidant. As **immigrant** college students, we saw him as the closest thing to a village elder in our lives. His replies, **"Yaap," "Fosho,"** and "I gotcha, bro," carried the weight of understanding in his own language.

They were a silent promise to guard not just our cars but also our **hopes** and fears from late-night confessions. He rarely asked questions, and when he did, they were merely subtle setups for his next tale. Rashon's resourcefulness in turning a dire situation into a livelihood was a daily reminder of the **power of adaptability.**

Rashon's Resourcefulness

One frigid holiday eve, a wave of **car break-ins** swept through the neighborhood like a thief in the night. Under Rashon's vigilant watch, however, our old black sedan sat untouched, a solitary island in a sea of **shattered glass** and despair. After the incident, club-goers heard about Rashon's services and started trusting his watchful eyes for a fee. He quickly became the neighborhood's guardian of cars.

Within weeks, he had added **cigarettes** and chewing gum to his makeshift stand. I still remember the day he first laid out those items—the way his hands trembled ever so slightly, the flicker of pride in his eyes as customers eagerly snatched them up. He yelled joyfully to new customers, "Yaap, I gotcha!"

One night, as my drunk friends and I lingered, he chuckled,

"I should start charging ya'll for **therapy.**"

Though his eyes betrayed deep understanding, as another round of slurred confessions about broken hearts spilled into the smoky air.

His makeshift stand became more than a convenience store; it was a **sanctuary**. The crisis had turned some clubgoers' world upside down, yet he found a way to support us all, teaching me that even in the darkest times, there's a light to be found if you know where to look.

Rashon's ingenuity soon expanded his role from mere guardian to entrepreneur, adding small sales of cheap cologne to his watchful services. This shift demonstrated true **resourcefulness:** Thriving by recognizing and **seizing opportunities**, no matter the circumstance. Despite being homeless, Rashon's entrepreneurial spirit continued to roam.

Lessons in Adaptability

Rashon's story embodies a universal principle of resourcefulness and **adaptability**, showing us that we can find potential in situations many would dismiss as **hopeless**. By looking at our challenges through a new lens, we can discover opportunities for growth where we least expect them, reminding us that our current situation is not our final destination.

His journey from homelessness to entrepreneurship serves as both an **inspiration** and a roadmap for navigating life's challenges. Witnessing Rashon's success reminds me that every obstacle can reveal a silver lining if we choose to see it. This insight has sparked a desire in me to chart my own path of ingenuity and **adaptability.**

Personal Reflection

Sometimes, you have to be willing to look silly while pursuing success or growth. Think about Rashon's journey—he went from being homeless to becoming a **successful entrepreneur.** Watching Rashon succeed against all odds stirred something deep within me. I felt a surge of determination, **a burning desire** to transform my own setbacks into stepping stones. I decided to apply for a mailroom job at a local firm—an opportunity I initially believed was beyond my reach due to my **lack of typing** experience.

To my surprise, this position not only led me to discover other opportunities within the firm but also served as a catalyst for **elevating** my career in corporate America. Let Rashon's adaptability inspire you as well.

Similarly, during the pandemic, I began posting inspirational videos on social media. Some friends and relatives thought I was being silly; others even **ridiculed** me, saying social media was for teenagers. Little did they know those videos would become the catalyst for writing this book.

Now, think about your own life. What situation are you **overlooking** as an opportunity for growth? Remember, if anyone truly understood your calling, it would've been a conference call. Your journey is unique to you. Is there a challenge you're **avoiding** because of the fear of **looking foolish?** Reflect on Rashon's story and my experiences. Consider how you can apply these lessons to your own journey.

Reflecting on Rashon's ingenuity, here are some actionable lessons I've learned that you can start applying today:

- **Reflect & Reframe**: Write down some challenges or mundane routines at work or home and consider how you can turn them into opportunities for growth.

- **Share & Inspire**: Discuss your steps and goals with your trusted circle. This not only reinforces your resolve but also spreads inspiration.

- **Visualize Success**: Imagine the impact of your actions on your life. Even minor adjustments can pave the way for significant achievements. Research shows that when you visualize your goals in vivid detail, your brain interprets it as real, helping to build the **confidence** and neural pathways needed to achieve them.

Remember, we can't always choose the music life plays for us, but we can choose **how we dance to it**. "Yaap, fosho, life got you."

Nairobi's Baguette Lesson: Understanding Readiness

A Taste of France in Eastlands

Growing up in Nairobi's Eastlands, Chef Mwangi, a family friend, brought the essence of a **French bakery** into our home. His rich laughter and vivid tales complemented the buttery scents wafting from the oven. The sizzle of pans and the rhythmic chopping of vegetables created a symphony in our small kitchen, turning every meal into an event. With a unique *je ne sais quoi*, he transformed our simple meals of **Muthokoi**, Githeri, and **Chapati** into culinary adventures.

The Apron and the Lesson

Chef Mwangi was more than just a family friend; he was like an uncle to us. His apron, always slightly dusted with flour, felt soft and comforting in my small hands, and I loved the rustle of the fabric as he moved around the kitchen. I loved to wear his apron, especially when my sister's friends visited, always drawing **compliments** and evoking their senses. It was my magic charm. He sparked my **curiosity** about life beyond our city's borders and taught us the importance of **timing** and readiness in all things.

A Baguette's Unexpected Journey

One Easter, Chef Mwangi introduced us to crusty, long French bread. "They're called baguettes," he said after our initial shock and wonder. In our neighborhood, alive with Swahili chatter and street food aromas, these baguettes were as foreign as snow. My cousin poked one, half-expecting it to speak French. This amusing encounter reminded me of the **new experiences** that readiness allows us to embrace.

Eager to share, my mother suggested we give some to our neighbor, Mrs. Abeba. She often shared stories of her **Ethiopian** homeland, along with the rich traditions and flavors of its cuisine. However, the next day, I found our precious baguettes **discarded** in her trash bucket near the door. The sight stopped me cold—crumbs mingling with discarded scraps, their once golden crust dulled by grime. Confusion, hurt, and anger surged through me, a painful reminder that not everyone is ready to receive what we offer.

I couldn't help but wonder—was it the **taste** or something deeper that led her to discard them? The urge to rescue them, to wipe away the dust and restore their former glory, was overwhelming. Yet the bread remained untouched, a silent testament to the chasm between our worlds. As I stood there, Mrs. Abeba walked by, and I couldn't hold it anymore.

"Why did you trash the bread?" I demanded, **disappointment** evident in my tone, shocked at my own courage and newfound love for this baguette.

"That bread was so hard even a dog wouldn't eat it. Please don't offer your neighbors stale bread again."

I was ready to **defend** the honor of our offering. "They're called baguettes. And it's French bread," I replied, crossing my arms and glaring at her.

"Bagutt? Are you sure it's bread?" she responded, her lips curling into a bemused smile as she shook her head, the very idea seeming absurd to her. I sighed and walked away.

Reflecting on these moments, I **painfully** realized Mrs. Abeba wasn't ready for our **gifts.** Her rejection taught me more about human nature than I expected. I learned that readiness is crucial for both giving and receiving.

Remember, if someone isn't ready to accept your offering, it doesn't **diminish the value** of the gift or your generosity. It simply means the timing isn't right. Reflecting on this lesson, I came to understand the importance of emotional and mental preparation in welcoming new experiences and perspectives.

As I pondered these experiences, I came to understand a profound truth. The most beautiful things in life are not things. They are people, places, memories, and pictures. They are feelings, moments, smiles, and laughter.

If I miss a gift, I remind myself that maybe I wasn't ready or it wasn't meant for me. I've learned to move on without any **regrets,** knowing that what's meant for me will always find me, no matter how long it might take. We all face times when our offerings aren't ready to be embraced. It's essential to consider the **readiness** of both the giver and the receiver. This understanding helps me trust the timing of life, knowing that when both **hearts are ready,** the right opportunities will align perfectly.

Just like a well-intentioned baguette, some things in life require the right timing and preparation to be fully **appreciated.** When considering the "baguette" you're offering or receiving, ask yourself: Is the timing right? Is the person you're gifting ready to receive it?

111

What's the risk in "tasting" something new, and are you prepared to savor it?

These questions guide me now, ensuring I am as ready to give as I am to receive, embracing each new experience with an **open heart** and mind. After all, just as a perfectly baked baguette finds its way to the right hands, what's truly meant for you will always find you.

"Those who get angry when you set a boundary are the ones you need to set boundaries for."
– Brene Brown

Manipulation Beyond Borders: Abiola's Path to Liberation

A Lesson Beyond Books

In the heart of lush, sprawling **East Texas,** my college experience was illuminated by more than just textbooks and lectures; it was enriched by the diverse lives and stories that surrounded me. The remarkable people around me added to this richness. Among them stood **Abiola from Ghana.** His wildly unruly **"electric crown"** of wayward hair was a striking testament to his boundless energy and deeply rooted heritage. It was as if his thoughts were too expansive for his mind to contain.

Abiola wasn't just a student; he was a **living lesson**, showing us that in Ghana, hair is more than just style—it's a powerful connection to one's roots and culture. His vibrant hair was like a flag, boldly and defiantly signaling his heritage and **freedom** to the world.

Struggles and Sacrifices

But challenges shadowed Abiola's journey. To pay for his school fees, he juggled a part-time job moving furniture on weekends and sweeping the college compounds. Despite his efforts, the workload took its toll. Abiola occasionally **donated blood** for cash, adding another layer to his relentless determination to stay afloat.

"I can't believe I'm in America, and my own people are still bleeding me dry," he would sometimes say, his voice a mix of disbelief and resolve.

In moments of desperation, he'd half-jokingly ask, "Where can I sell my hair?"

His resolve was clear, but behind his smile lurked a quiet struggle. The fatigue was so overwhelming that he often found himself sleeping through classes, missing crucial lectures.

Family Pressure and Manipulation

Abiola's interactions with his **family** back in Ghana were fraught with **tension.** Each conversation added a new layer of stress, making it harder for him to focus on his studies. The increasing demands from home compounded his worries, but he rarely spoke about them. One evening, during a late-night study session, he finally opened up.

"Now they blame me for **empty hands** after all the money I've sent home," he quipped, though there was no humor in his eyes. "Their lies make me feel useless."

He shared vivid stories of **manipulation** from his family back home, making him feel spellbound and questioning his reality. These constant demands for money wove a web of guilt and financial strain around him.

114

He recounted a phone call from his mother.

"Abiola, your sister needs money for her school fees," she said, her voice a mix of urgency and expectation.

"You've been away for so long, and we are struggling."

His heart sank as he realized he had to **choose** between his own needs and his family's endless demands.

The Breaking Point

As the demands grew, the stress began to take a toll on Abiola's health. He fell ill, his once bright demeanor dimming, and his face now long and mournful. His academic performance suffered, and he eventually lost his part-time job—the only way he could pay his school fees. He was unraveling. The **web of guilt** and obligation seemed inescapable.

The pressure of having to stay in **visa status** meant he couldn't take a semester off, further exacerbating his situation. With no health insurance, he couldn't seek medical help and had to rely on over-the-counter medicines. This added to his sense of helplessness and isolation.

"These people will finish me!" he exclaimed one evening, frustration etched on his face. Light gone from his eyes.

"This life... it's just not worth it." The words barely escaped his trembling lips.

"Where can I find a witch doctor who doesn't need health insurance?"

His voice, usually strong and resilient, now sounded **fragile**.

Reflecting on Our Own Lives

Abiola's challenges with his family's expectations raise a broader question: Have you ever felt trapped by others' demands, as if under a spell that distorts your sense of self? Abiola's journey, though unique, echoes a common struggle. It reminds us how expectations can entangle us, blurring the lines between love and control.

Abiola's story illustrates how even families thousands of miles away can still impact our mental health. In such situations, it's important to remember that while you can't always change your close relatives around you, you can choose the path you take.

Finding Freedom

The turning point in Abiola's journey came **unexpectedly.** One day, he **lost his phone**, the primary tether to his family's demands.

"That phone saved my life from these people!" he said, relief washing over his face.

This period of silence became his **sanctuary,** a chance to see the web for what it was. He deliberately delayed buying another phone, sharing the new number only with trusted friends, carefully avoiding the demands that once ensnared him.

During this period, he found solace in nature, often taking long walks in the nearby park. **"For the first time, I felt free,"** he shared with me one afternoon as we sat under a towering pecan tree, the darkness swelling angrily at our backs.

"I realized I had to reclaim my life."

With a newfound bounce in his step and fading shadows under his eyes, he decided to cut his hair. Each lock falling to the floor

116

represented a visible weight lifted from his shoulders. Finally. His smooth, hairless head shone with a liberated light, a testament to his newfound freedom. As he watched the last strand fall, he felt the webs of guilt and obligation that had **trapped** him unravel, leaving him lighter and ready to embrace his new beginning.

Taking Control of Our Responses

Abiola realized he couldn't change what was happening, so he chose to control his response. This prompts us to reflect on our own lives: Where might we need to cut away our **tangled webs**? As Shaista Saba wisely said, "Walk away from people who put you down. Walk away from trying to please people who will never see your worth. The more you walk away from things that poison your soul, the healthier you will be."

The Power of Saying No

Abiola's journey teaches us the importance of saying "No" to regain control and honor our self-worth. It's a poignant reminder to **love yourself** because, if we don't, we'll always seek others to fill the void within us—a void no one else can ever fill.

Establishing Clear Boundaries

Inspired by his bold decision to cut his hair and the fortuitous loss of his phone, consider how you can establish clear boundaries in your own life. This decisive action will empower you and mark a critical turning point in preserving your mental health and self-respect.

Affirming a Healthier You

Remember, setting boundaries isn't just about saying no to others—it's about affirming a healthier, more empowered you.

Abiola's story teaches us that true freedom begins with setting boundaries and valuing ourselves. Where can you start setting boundaries today to honor your **self-worth?**

Summary:

Life is brimming with opportunities waiting to be recognized and seized. In this section, the stories and lessons emphasize the importance of keen perception and bold action. We explore how recognizing potential in unexpected places and moments can open doors to new possibilities. Additionally, we delve into the subtle art of distinguishing genuine opportunities from manipulative traps. Through these narratives, we learned that seizing opportunities often requires courage, creativity, and the wisdom to say no when necessary. These insights inspire us to remain vigilant and proactive, transforming opportunities into tangible achievements while safeguarding our integrity and autonomy.

Part V:
Embracing Identity and Self-Worth

In a world that often pressures us to conform to **external expectations** and societal standards, discovering and embracing our true selves can be a challenging yet deeply rewarding endeavor. "Embracing Identity and Self-Worth" delves into the heart of what it means to recognize our **intrinsic value** and honor our individuality. This theme invites readers on a transformative journey towards self-acceptance, encouraging them to look within and find strength in their unique qualities.

"The world breaks everyone; afterward, some are strong in the broken places."
–Ernest Hemmingway

Echoes of Marcus:
Village Education

The Arrival

He introduced himself as Marcus, his voice full of confidence as if he were **untouchable.** His laughter and charisma instantly filled the room. He stood tall and broad, **a giant among men,** casting a long shadow that demanded respect. He carried with him a **foreign scent,** an exotic blend of cologne and the faint aroma of cities far away, mingling with the sweat of his journey. Yet in our **close-knit village,** he was like a sequoia among maples—majestic, yet undeniably out of place.

He proudly dubbed himself "**Halfrican-American**," a term that sounded as grand as a movie title to my ten-year-old ears. He had traced his father to our village, but it was too late—his father had already **passed away**. Back then, Marcus seemed larger than life in our small village, a towering figure of confidence and charm. But beneath this confident exterior, there were **hidden layers** we were yet to see.

Vulnerability Unveiled

The once invincible Marcus began to show cracks in the armor that shielded his heart. One day, his laughter, usually a room-filling sound, **echoed hollowly,** leaving an uneasy silence in its wake. Something was different. His eyes, usually bright with **confidence**, dimmed for a moment as he glanced away, his smile not quite reaching them.

One evening, he shared stories of searching for the father he never knew. His voice, always steady and sure, wavered like a leaf in the wind. The confident aura he always carried seemed to waver, replaced by a moment of **vulnerability**. For the first time, his shoulders slumped, losing their usual strength.

"He moved to Kenya before I was born,"

Marcus said, his voice dropping to a whisper as he stared into his drink. The flicker of the fire cast shadows on his face, reflecting the **turmoil within.**

"It feels like I'm drifting, searching for a place to call home."

His fingers tightening around the glass as if it were the only thing keeping him anchored.

Contributions and Questions

As the days passed, Marcus faced challenges adjusting to the **local customs** and lifestyle in our village. I remember the first time he had to use a **pit latrine.** I handed him a newspaper. He chuckled, his voice tinged with amusement,

"I don't read newspapers in the toilet," he said.

I laughed and showed him how to rub the paper between his hands.

"It's to make it softer, like tissue paper." He looked at the newspaper skeptically but followed my lead.

Mzee Muli, an elder known for his wisdom, took a particular interest in Marcus. **"Our son,"** he said one evening by the fire,

"adapting takes time. Your father had the same struggles."

Marcus nodded. "Thank you for your guidance, Mzee Muli. Sometimes, it feels like I'm trying to fit into a puzzle piece where I don't belong."

Mzee Muli smiled. "Belonging isn't about fitting perfectly; it's about understanding and respecting. It's better to try, so just give it time."

Drawing on his military background, Marcus financed and helped construct a well as a gesture of **gratitude.** The village presented him with a **prized spear** in gratitude for bringing life to the community. At night, under the vast African sky, he would sit by the campfire, his usually commanding voice softened with introspection.

"Here, they call me a soldier," he confided, his gaze fixed on the distant horizon. His breath hitched, losing its steady rhythm with the weight of his words.

"Back home… I'm nobody." He took a swig from his flask, his eyes momentarily closing as if trying to drown the uncertainty. When he continued, his voice was barely a whisper. **"Where do I fit in?"**

He was warned against drinking *"Chang'aa"* a local illicit brew and staying out late because of the unpredictable **wild animals.**

"You don't have to drink to belong, Marcus," the elder advised gently.

"I'm a grown man, and I've survived many wars. I guess I'm still trying to figure out where I belong," Marcus replied, staring into his cup with a sad smile.

"You are one of us. Your **father's spirit lives** within us." Another villager added.

Marcus's eyes softened. "Thank you. I think I'll just have soup tonight," Marcus replied, nodding respectfully to the elders, his smile a shadow of its former self.

The Tragedy

When Marcus vanished during Christmas 1990, whispers of worry spread like wildfire. Days passed with no sign of him. Then came the **dreadful news**—he had been found near the main road, grievously injured. A **leopard** had torn through his flesh, leaving him barely recognizable. Half of his face was a brutal testament to the savage attack. The sight was horrifying, a stark contrast to the vibrant, confident man he once was.

As the news rippled through the village, *"Wuuuwi! Wuuuwi!"* they wailed, their mournful cries rising in a haunting chorus that echoed off the hills, carrying the weight of their collective sorrow. It was as if a dark cloud had descended.

The village quickly rallied, pooling resources for his medical bills and ensuring he was never alone. Elders, including the village **witch doctor**, Kilonzo, took turns by his bedside, demonstrating their deep concern and **commitment.** One of the elders, Mzee Muli, and Koki, the witch doctor's daughter, were among those who spent long hours by Marcus's side, holding his hand and offering words of comfort.

"Marcus, you are strong. You will heal," Mzee Muli whispered, his voice full of unwavering belief.

"You can't cure American evil spirits,"

Marcus rasped weakly, his voice barely more than a whisper.

His once vibrant eyes were now clouded with pain and resignation. The air was thick with the smell of herbs and smoke. Hopeless. The witch doctor rubbed **charcoal and chicken blood** on his forehead, invoking ancient blessings to cleanse him of any evils that might have clung to him from the shadows of the attack. To Marcus, **the rituals** felt as foreign as the land itself, yet he lay still, too weak to resist, too lost in his own despair to argue.

A Question of Belonging

In the quiet nights that followed, Marcus would sit by the flickering campfire, staring into the flames as if seeking answers.

"Can I truly belong here, or do I just exist between the lines?" he wondered aloud one evening, his voice barely more than a whisper.

As the words escaped him, his face contorted in a mix of pain and doubt, **the scars** from his ordeal twisting with the raw emotion beneath. The question hung heavy in the air, weighted with his yearning for a place to call home. The villagers, though silent, felt the weight of his words and the fragility of his newfound strength.

The Final Incident

Just a few months later, this precarious balance was shattered. Marcus was fatally injured by a **stray bull elephant** that charged him unexpectedly near the well. The impact knocked him into the murky waters where, tragically, he **drowned.** A cruel twist of fate. The same waters he had once blessed the village with, bringing life and sustenance, ultimately claimed his own. In those murky depths, the village lost not just a man but a **symbol of resilience and hope,** leaving a void that could never be filled.

The village mourned the loss of their **"Halfrican American"** son, who had taught them invaluable lessons. He was ceremoniously buried next to his father's grave with his prized spear, a symbol of the strength and **courage** he carried within him, which was now passed on to the next generation.

Amid the mourning, Koki, the witch doctor's daughter, revealed she was carrying Marcus's child. The village fell into **stunned silence,** the weight of her words hanging in the air like a heavy mist. Slowly, as the reality sank in, the silence gave way to a murmur—a **mix of sorrow** for the man they lost and hope for the life he left behind. This news, while sorrowful, also brought a glimmer of hope and continuity to the grieving community.

"He will live on through his child," the chief declared, his voice breaking, "and we will honor him by caring for his blood."

Reflections and Lessons

As kids, we thought he was **untouchable**, so we were shocked to learn of his death. The news left me deeply saddened. Marcus's journey, filled with triumphs and heartache, teaches us a powerful lesson: **respect for new environments** is essential. His story shows that true adaptation comes from **empathy and humility**. Every community holds unique wisdom, and by embracing these differences, we can turn personal challenges into opportunities for communal growth and renewal.

Applying Marcus's Lessons:

When entering a new environment, take time to **learn** and respect local customs. Approach new experiences with empathy and humility. Listen deeply. **Engage** with the community actively. Contribute meaningfully by identifying and addressing **community needs** with your skills and resources. Reflect on how you can build "wells" in your own life—actions that bring life and sustenance to those around you. These actions might be kindness, support, or sharing knowledge and skills.

Conclusion

As I navigate my own **journey** in the U.S., I often think of Marcus and the profound lessons his life taught me about the importance of empathy, humility, and meaningful contribution. His life prompts us to ask: How can we **honor** the communities we join with respect and humility?

As you step into your next new environment, take a moment to consider how you can **apply** these lessons today and begin building those wells that will bring life and sustenance to your new community.

How are you currently adding value to your local community? What actions can you take to make a positive impact today?

"The brave man is not he who does not feel afraid, but he who conquers that fear."
— Nelson Mandela.

Voice Unchained:
A Journey from Silence to Liberation

Harmony's Illusion

For years, my voice was a **prisoner to silence**, chained by the belief that speaking up was a painful act. This silence was my shield, my illusion of harmony. Throughout my personal and professional life, I chose silence over confrontation, believing this **suppression** was a noble sacrifice for peace.

Roots of Silence

Deeply **rooted** in my African childhood, this habit shaped me profoundly. Back home, children were expected to be seen and not heard unless spoken to. Strict elders were often nicknamed **"Mkoloni,"** referencing the British **colonial** influence that emphasized strictness and conformity.

We learned early on that our voices were best kept low, our **opinions tucked away**, and our only words of response—"yes sir" or "yes mom"—echoed like a mantra through the halls of our childhood. In school, we followed orders without question. We knew that any attempt to challenge authority could result in swift and harsh **corporal punishment**.

During a major tribal meeting, my heart pounded as I suggested,

"We should all get milk and bread" as a reward for helping prepare the meeting.

Silence hung in the air for a moment, as if my words had broken some unspoken rule, the elders' stern faces betraying no reaction. For a heartbeat or two, I thought I might faint. I realized then, the weight of my small rebellion—the **quiet audacity of a child** daring to speak out.

In our community, food was considered a reward for good deeds. I hoped this simple offering on behalf of the other kids would be well-received. Yet, it was deeply **disrespectful** to speak to the elders, let alone make demands during such an important gathering. In that moment, I became a rebel. I had crossed an invisible line, and there was no going back.

Swiftly, I was sent to harvest maize with the workers, a clear reminder of the cultural boundaries I had **overstepped**. As I moved through the tall, rustling stalks, my face burned—not from the midday sun, but from the sting of my own mistake. I had thought my words were just, that my intentions were noble. But now, the labor wasn't just tiring; it was a **penance.**

I heard the children's laughter ripple through the field, sharp and mocking, each taunt a fresh wound. Unbelievable. I felt embarrassed and regretful. A cold doubt settled in my chest. That day, the sting of my mistake went beyond the physical labor. It solidified the lesson that **questioning authority**, even with good intentions, could bring shame and ostracism. As I worked, the weight of my **mistake** pressed heavily on me.

In that scorching sun, I learned a bitter lesson: My voice, when used, could bring **reprimand rather than respect**.

Carrying Silence across Borders

Even after moving to the United States, my **pattern of silence** persisted. In team meetings and personal interactions, I stayed quiet; at the gym, I stepped aside. Silence became my refuge. I avoided the spotlight, even when I had ideas that could have improved a project or resolved an issue at work. Each time I **chose silence,** a part of me felt **invisible**, but the fear of conflict kept my mouth shut. If there were an award for silence, I'd accept it with a nod and a quiet smile.

Liberation and Reflection

But a turning point came one **Easter Sunday** at small African church. As a volunteer tasked with arranging chairs, I meticulously set each one in place. A fellow volunteer, always quick to direct others despite not being our team lead, started rearranging them, insisting he had a better layout.

Memories long buried beneath the sands of time resurfaced, striking me like a sharp, unexpected gust of wind. The storm within me was about to erupt as I clenched my fists and bit my lip. I could feel years of **suppressed frustration** boiling over. My heart pounded in my chest, each beat echoing the rage that surged through my veins. Finally, I couldn't hold back any longer—my voice, raw and unrestrained, tore through the stillness of the **church.**

"What the heck are you doing?" I yelled, the words bouncing off the walls and shattering the hymns of renewal.

131

A heavy, **suffocating silence** followed. The faces around me blurred as I stood there, my outstretched hands trembling. I could see a woman in the front row clutching her **Bible** tighter, her eyes wide with shock. A child's gaze flickered between me and his mother, unsure and frightened.

Guilt washed over me, my face burned with embarrassment. I glanced down at my feet, and I couldn't meet anyone's eyes. The weight of their stares pressed down on me. But amidst the shame, a surprising sense of **liberation** crept in, like a soft whisper in the back of my mind, subtle yet undeniable. This was church, after all—a place of forgiveness, where one could lay bare their soul without fear of **condemnation.**

In the silence that followed, I took a deep breath. As the tension eased, a strange clarity emerged. I realized that breaking my silence, even awkwardly, was a **crucial** first step towards change. The incident brought **relief** and sparked a deeper transformation in my approach to communication.

Confronting Fears

After that incident in church, emboldened by my newfound freedom, I decided to confront my **loud neighbor**. Summoning my courage, I knocked on his door, ready for a difficult conversation. I stood there, stunned, noticing he was packing. My prepared words evaporated. The boxes and open suitcase mocked my rehearsed speech.

As we exchanged pleasantries, I felt a sense of **irony.** Perhaps God was teaching me a lesson in timing. The dreaded confrontation became a simple, cordial exchange.

A New Beginning

Reflecting on that day, I understood something crucial about myself and the nature of true peace and **assertiveness.** That church incident, though jarring, became a **turning point**, not just a moment of outburst. It was a catalyst for change, signaling the beginning of my journey towards reclaiming my voice.

I realized that peace is not merely the **absence of conflict** but the presence of authentic self-expression. Interacting with my neighbor reminded me that it's important to choose our battles carefully.

Recognizing Patterns

Recognizing the pattern of silence in my professional life, I made a conscious effort to change. From that day forward, I started to **challenge** my habit of silence actively. In professional settings, I began to **voice my ideas** and concerns during meetings despite the initial discomfort.

My heart would race, and my palms would sweat, but each instance of speaking up built **my confidence** incrementally. I discovered that some of my colleagues valued my input while others saw it as a threat. This validation reinforced my newfound assertiveness.

Personal Growth

In my personal life, I practiced speaking up with friends and family. Expressing my needs and desires directly **transformed** my relationships. Some strained under the weight of my honesty, but others deepened, creating more meaningful connections. I realized that **speaking my truth** not only alleviated internal stress but also fostered mutual respect and understanding.

The journey was challenging, but the rewards were profound. Along the way, I learned that you can still be kind even if you disagree with someone. Be aware that some people might perceive you as **being argumentative,** even when you respectfully speak your mind. Remember to avoid getting drawn into endless debates. Others might be battling their own inner conflicts. True growth is when someone tries to provoke the old you but can no longer find that person.

Inspired by my personal transformation, I developed **practical steps** to help others break their silence. By identifying issues, preparing thoughts, and actively listening, anyone can begin their journey to self-expression.

Reflection and Action

Step 1: Identify and Assess the Issue

- **Identify the Issue**: Take a moment to define what's bothering you clearly. For instance, if you feel overlooked at work, specify the situations where this happens. Ask yourself questions like, "When do I feel most ignored?" or "What specific actions by others make me feel undervalued?"

- **Reflect on Past Experiences**: Recall a moment when you chose silence over speaking up. What were the circumstances, and how did it make you feel? Who was **present** when this happened?

Step 2: Prepare Your Thoughts

- *Write Down Your Thoughts*: Write down what you want to say and practice it. Rehearse in front of a mirror or with a friend.

- *Choose the Right Time*: Select the appropriate time to speak up. Timing your words carefully, such as speaking during a scheduled meeting rather than spontaneously, can significantly affect outcomes.

- *Ask Open-Ended Questions:* This might involve asking open-ended questions like, "Can you tell me more about why you feel this way?" or "How do you think we can address this issue together?" By actively listening and showing empathy, you can foster a more constructive and collaborative dialogue.

Continuous Improvement

Think about the times you stayed silent—what steps could you take today towards **speaking your truth**? Our voices aren't just tools; they're testimonies to our existence, capable of creating harmony. Don't be discouraged if change doesn't happen right away. Every small step you take builds your confidence and effectiveness.

Remember, this is a lifetime practice as you evolve and grow.

Bear in mind that whatever you **lose** by speaking up isn't a loss but an **alignment.** Embrace the power of your voice today, and begin your journey towards a more authentic and fulfilling life. Speak up to keep the peace within you rather than staying silent and letting chaos take root.

"Hello, Hello":
The Power of Names and Identity

A Grandfather's Legacy

When I was a young boy, my **late grandfather** returned from Europe, a figure of unmatched elegance in our village. He was always clad in a tailored European suit, and exuded an effortless sophistication. His confident posture and panther-like strides commanded attention. A man of substance.

Every morning, he greeted us with a booming "**Hellooo!**" In our tribal dialect, **Kamba**, which has no "H," his greeting became "Allooo"—a sound that vibrated through our homestead, filling me with **pride** and admiration. As he moved, the fabric of his Kaunda suits whispered gently, and the faint lingering scent of a foreign cigar added to his enigmatic presence.

The Significance of a Nickname

Over time, this affectionate mispronunciation soon became more than a nickname; it became his **identity**. As a child, I believed "Allooo" was his real name, thinking my grandfather had the coolest name. But in high school, when I stumbled upon his birth certificate and discovered his actual name—**William Mbaluka Mwengi.** I was stunned. I felt a mix of surprise and a deeper connection to the man I had always known as "Allooo." It was as though I was seeing a new facet of a familiar gemstone, the same man yet somehow more complex.

That nickname had woven itself into my perception of him, showing how names, even when **altered**, can profoundly shape our sense of self. Reflecting on this story prompts us to consider how names shape our **perceptions**. What comes to mind when you hear your name? Are there any mix-ups or unique stories?

Navigating Cultural Differences

For my grandfather, "Allooo" symbolized a joyful welcome, embraced fully by him. It was more than a name. His name radiated positivity, making him a beacon of **influence.** He was the man who planted all the trees that provided shade for the local women in our market. This personal connection highlights how names can influence our identity and the way others perceive us.

While common names like **Catherine or Patricia** often have well-known nicknames, it's important to remember that assuming a nickname without someone's permission can be disrespectful. **Mispronunciations** of my last name, Mwengi, have led to amusing errors like "Wengie" or "Mengii."

Once, our secretary called me **"Wedgie,"** and not correcting her felt like losing a small but important piece of myself. It was like my **identity** was slipping away, leaving me like a faceless torso. This experience isn't unique to me.

I remember the first time I tried to pronounce **"Nguyen"** during a group project in college. My tongue stumbled, turning it into a garbled mess. The awkward silence that followed was a stark reminder of how much weight a name carries. Names like "Bang Ho," "Fu Xuan," and "Hei Muer" have also tripped my tongue, each mispronunciation a small but meaningful misstep.

These struggles emphasize the universal experience of navigating cultural differences and how names are central to our identity and perception. Whether real or nicknames, mispronunciations can often be more than a simple mistake; they can feel like a **misrecognition** of one's identity and heritage.

Embracing Our Names and Legacies

Adding humor to the mix, in college, I had a friend named **Ben Dover.** His name was the source of endless **jokes** and puns, but it also gave him a unique identity. While some might see it as a burden, Ben embraced his name with good humor, turning potential ridicule into a memorable trait. This shows how our reactions to names, even humorous or unusual ones, shape our personal narratives.

Mispronounced or ridiculed names can cause embarrassment and impact self-esteem. In professional settings, frequent mispronunciations may make someone feel **undervalued**. Socially, names influence first impressions and connections. And let's not even talk about **AI auto correction** of names, a source of endless frustration. Names Matter. Correcting someone's pronunciation of your name affirms your identity and personal story.

This mutual respect is vital, urging us to value names as part of our heritage. Names **bridge cultures** worldwide. Consider "Sakura" in Japan, echoing cherry blossom beauty, or "Adebayo" in Nigeria, meaning "the crown meets joy."

Our names reflect our stories, grounding us in our cultural and familial backgrounds. The **respect** and understanding of names across cultures highlight the universal significance of names in shaping identity.

Even with life's changes, the essence of our names persists. In my tribe's naming traditions, a boy born at night is named **"Mutuku,"** meaning "the night," while a girl born during a famine is named **"Kamene,"** meaning "unloved." Recognizing these traditions shows how names immortalize deeds, underscoring how actions define legacies. In summary, names encapsulate our heritage, stories, and identities, carrying the weight of **our histories.** Embracing their significance helps us appreciate the rich tapestry of human experience and fosters mutual respect.

Have you ever mispronounced a name? What was that like for you? In exploring these questions, what tales does your name hold?

Sharing the story of your name with someone can deepen **connections** and celebrate our diverse cultural backgrounds. Names hold power. They are not just labels but carry our histories and identities. Embracing our identity and self-worth is a profound journey of self-acceptance and empowerment. Reflecting on the moments when names were **mispronounced,** either my own or others, has made me more mindful of this journey.

Is there a name you purposely refuse to honor?

By sharing and respecting the **stories behind our names**, we celebrate the rich tapestry of our diverse cultural backgrounds. In doing so, this mutual respect fosters deeper connections and enriches our shared human experience.

Well, "Hellooo," what's your name?

Summary:

In this section, the stories and lessons highlight the **importance of understanding and valuing who we are**. Through personal anecdotes and diverse narratives, we explore the myriad paths to recognizing our unique strengths and embracing our true selves. These stories reveal how **self-worth** is not defined by external validation but by our own inner recognition of our value. Through these insights, we are inspired to honor our identities, **celebrate** our individuality, and cultivate a deep sense of self-respect and confidence

Part VI:
Workplace Dynamics and Personal Boundaries

Discover the secrets to thriving in your professional life by mastering the art of workplace interactions and setting personal boundaries. This section provides valuable insights into building respectful relationships, communicating effectively, and maintaining your well-being. Learn how to safeguard your time and energy while balancing teamwork with assertiveness, leading to a more productive and satisfying work environment."

"Some people will only love you as much as they can use you. Their loyalty ends where the benefits stop."
— honeya

Outsmarting the Cuckoo:
Strategies for Handling Workplace Slackers

Navigating the Workplace "Cuckoos"

Ever wondered about the term "cuckoo"? Picture the cuckoo bird, **Cuculus canorus**, as the **James Bond** of the bird world, slyly infiltrating nests across Europe, Asia, and Africa. Infamous for their scandalous behavior, the birds lay eggs in the nests of unsuspecting birds like Dunnocks.

Male cuckoos are the ultimate slackers, ditching parental duties. Females abandon their **eggs,** opting for moonlit parties, intoxicating nectar, and rendezvous with exotic strangers. These **"brood parasites"** are nature's con artists.

Similarly, some people in our professional lives exhibit these behaviors.

Personal Experience: A College Lesson

I first encountered this "cuckoo" behavior in college, and boy, was it a wild ride. My roommate Jake led a research project focused on renewable energy solutions. This project required extensive collaboration and data analysis with a group of international students. Their first meeting resembled a comedy show—faces pale with anxiety, eyes wide like startled owls in the night.

Much like the unsuspecting Dunnocks left to care for the cuckoo's offspring, the international students found themselves overwhelmed, grappling with the project's demands and the language barrier. They were drowning in uncertainty. Jake, however, was no **slacker.** Stepping in where others hesitated, he became their knight in shining armor, ensuring the project didn't crumble under pressure. He'd taken on the role of the diligent dunnock, tirelessly tending to a nest that wasn't his.

Jake spent countless hours meticulously planning the project, **sacrificing** sleep and social time. Confident in his team's preparation, Jake left detailed instructions before visiting his sick mother out of state, hoping they would follow through in his absence. The nest seemed secure, it's foundation strong—at least, that's what he believed.

Upon his return, exhausted but relieved, Jake discovered that his team had presented the project without him during the finals. Since he wasn't present, he received an "incomplete" grade. His face twisted in disbelief and anger as the **betrayal** hit hard. Jake felt isolated and undervalued.

"No way," he muttered, his voice trembling with a mix of disbelief and anger. "They did this without me? After all the work I put in?"

He stared blankly at the empty room, his mind racing, his fingers curled into fists.

"Was I really just a stepping stone for them?"

The **betrayal** gnawed at him, a stark reminder of how easily people could turn their backs, just like those **cunning cuckoo** birds. Astonishing. A **bitter taste** filled his mouth as the reality sank in— he had been cast aside without a second thought. This wasn't just a minor setback; it was a soul-crushing revelation about the **fickle nature of teamwork.** Something Jake had always feared but never wanted to believe.

Recognizing and Addressing "Cuckoo" Behavior

Just as cuckoos **dump their burdens** on others, some colleagues might expect you to carry their projects to completion without giving you **credit.** Recognizing these behaviors is the first step in addressing them. Here are some practical steps:

- **Document Your Contributions:** Keep a detailed record of your work. Save emails, create a project journal, or use collaborative tools that timestamp contributions.

- **Promote Dialogue:** Approach the person involved with questions to foster dialogue rather than conflict. Channel your inner diplomat—calm, collected, and clear.

- **Seek Higher Authority:** If the behavior continues, talk to a supervisor. Present your documented evidence and suggest solutions.

- **Clarify Roles Early**: From the start, ensure that roles and responsibilities are clearly defined to avoid confusion.

Embracing Resilience and Inclusivity

Sometimes, letting it go and letting them revel in your work might be the best they can achieve on their own. Consider it as a **future blessing** in disguise—an opportunity to focus on your own growth and rise above. Maintain a positive attitude and focus on your growth and contributions. Just as the Dunnocks persistently call to protect what's theirs, we, too, can voice our strengths clearly and consistently, ensuring we are heard.

Final Thoughts

Remember, success built on perseverance and respect endures. Rise above challenges, uphold your values, and let your dedication and **integrity shine.** In the end, those qualities are what define true success and lasting teamwork. Just as a bird's nest stands strong through winds and storms. True teamwork prevails.

"Help someone, you earn a friend. Help someone too much, you make an enemy."
enemy."
– Erol Ozan

Say No to Baggage:
Reclaiming Your Life and Boundaries

Personal Chauffeur

Think about your own life. When was the last time you regretted saying "yes"? How did that anxiety and frustration impact your stress levels and overall happiness? I know this feeling all too well. Once, I found myself **trapped** in the role of a **personal driver** for a relative who frequently traveled back to Kenya on business trips.

Despite my own mounting responsibilities, I reluctantly said "yes" to her incessant requests, feeling the **imbalance** in our relationship deepen. Each trip, her luggage bloomed like a garden of weeds, spreading uncontrollably. It choked out **my own needs.** My desires vanished, swallowed by her endless demands.

At the **airport** check-in, she effortlessly handled each bag while my anxiety mounted. She tried to guilt the airline crew with desperate pleas: "My kids in Africa need these items badly," or her favorite line, "God will bless you for understanding."

A knot tightened in my stomach as I realized the high cost of avoiding tough conversations. The physical strain of her **deceptively heavy bags** mirrored the larger, unsustainable choices in my life—highlighting the futility of always saying "yes."

Emotional Toll

Each forced smile chipped away at my authenticity. It felt hollow and **resentful.** As a father, I recognized the critical need to prioritize and learn to say "no." Each time I said "yes" to others, I effectively said "no" to my family and myself. **Chronic stress** from overcommitting manifested in headaches and fatigue, further emphasizing the need for change.

Understanding Limits

We often say "yes" out of fear of **disappointing others**. Just as airplanes have luggage limits for safety and weight calculations, we, too, must recognize and respect our personal boundaries. When we exceed these limits, we risk emotional turbulence or, worse, a crash landing in your personal life.

Like airline workers who firmly reject extra luggage, it's important to stand firm when others try to bring their baggage into your life. **Weigh** it carefully and ensure you don't exceed your own limits. Have you ever found yourself agreeing to something, not out of genuine desire, but out of fear—**fear of conflict**, fear of letting someone down?

The First "No"

For me, the consequences were all too real. When I first said "no," her reaction was sharp and immediate. Narrowing her eyes, she twisted her lips into a scowl.

"Remember, we grew up together in the village. We have to take care of each other," she said, her voice dripping with disapproval.

"Our ancestors would be ashamed of you for saying no to your relative." Her words cut deep, reminding me of our **shared past**.

Just like the airline workers who firmly said "no" to excess baggage, I had to stand my ground. I felt torn between guilt and newfound self-respect. Guilt was her brush, painting me as **unhelpful and selfish.** Each stroke etched our shared history into my conscience.

Her **accusation** sparked a gradual awakening within me, making me wonder, "Am I really the villain, or am I finally honoring my boundaries?"

Despite pressure from her friends and some relatives, I stood my ground. I transitioned from guilt to cautious empowerment. Can you recall a time when you said "no" and felt both guilt and empowerment? How did it change your perspective?

Reflect on Your Life

Feeling trapped and frustrated, a pivotal question surfaced: "What if I start putting myself first?" The thought was both terrifying and exhilarating. **Terrifying** because it meant breaking free from the chains of others' expectations. **Exhilarating** because it hinted at the possibility of finally living on my own terms. This question was a turning point, a spark of rebellion against a life dictated by others.

Realizing your value and choosing your **own opinion** about yourself over others is crucial though it's easier said than done. As Erica Layne wisely said, "Balance isn't fitting everything in. It's starting with what's important and letting the rest fall as it will."

The Benefits of Saying "No"

Saying "no" profoundly impacts our mental health. It allows us to value ourselves more and prioritize our needs. This practice helps set boundaries and opens new opportunities. Saying "no" means saying "yes" to other parts of your life. **Self-care** includes taking space from people who stress you out. Listen to your **body's signals**: tension in your shoulders, fatigue, and irritability.

By consistently **enforcing your boundaries**, you reduce stress and anxiety, leading to a more balanced and fulfilling life. This also improves your relationships, as you engage with others from a place of respect and **self-assurance** rather than resentment. Don't let empathy for others drain you to the point where you can't show up for yourself.

Practical Steps

If you struggle with saying "no," **start small:** Decline one minor request this week. Be direct, using phrases like

"No, I can't." "I don't have the **emotional capacity** for that." "I don't want to." "This is out of my scope of expertise," or "I know my schedule is open, but I'm using it to rest."

Don't apologize or offer extensive reasons. **Don't lie**, as lying will likely lead to guilt—the very feeling you're trying to avoid. Be polite, saying, "Thanks for asking."

Reflect and Let Go

Observe how this small step lightens your load, like setting down heavy luggage. It's in these moments of lightness that you might find profound peace in living authentically. You might face **resistance** or guilt initially; isn't that just part of the journey toward growth? Remember every "no" makes room for new opportunities. Don't feel guilty for wanting to rest. Your value isn't tied to your ability to help others all the time.

Conclusion

Consider the burdens you're ready to **release** and what you need to keep. Imagine the liberation that you'll feel as you let go. It's about embracing freedom and opportunity. Begin your journey of saying "no" today; it's a powerful step that could open new horizons, allowing for greater joy and **fewer burdens.**

If you keep saying "yes" too often, you risk **overextending** yourself, potentially hindering your ability to achieve your full potential. Every decision to let go or hold on is a step toward a more **intentional life**.

Summary:

Navigating workplace dynamics and establishing personal boundaries are vital for professional and personal well-being. This section explores the complexities of professional relationships and the importance of clear boundaries. Effective communication, mutual respect, and self-awareness foster a harmonious work environment. Learn to protect your time, energy, and integrity amidst professional demands, balancing collaboration with assertiveness for a healthier, more fulfilling workplace experience.

Part VII:
Embracing Life's
Challenges and Lessons

Discover the transformative power of overcoming life's hurdles. From conquering **glossophobia** to practicing gratitude, embracing the joy of giving without expectations, and overcoming **cherophobia,** this theme delves into personal growth and resilience, offering insights into living fully and fearlessly.

"Courage is resistance to fear, mastery of fear-not absence of fear."
– Mark Twain

Oil Your Buttocks:
Conquering Glossophobia

The Challenge

During the sweltering summer of 2018, I was unexpectedly tasked with presenting our team's goals to the entire HR department. Until then, my only audience had been cattle I tended beneath the vast Kenyan skies. That was my **comfort zone.** The thought of standing before a room full of professionals, with my **Kenyan accent** exposed, filled me with crippling anxiety.

Glossophobia, the fear of public speaking, is one of the most common **phobias.** For me, it was more than a fear; it was a **paralyzing** dread that settled in my chest, squeezing the breath out of

157

me. Whenever a project or assignment hinted at speaking in front of a crowd, my mind raced for a **way out.**

I became skilled at concocting reasons to dodge the spotlight—feigning a sudden illness, volunteering for any behind-the-scenes tasks, even claiming a last-minute emergency. The mere thought of standing before a room full of people, their eyes fixed on me, was enough to make my palms sweat and my voice falter before I even opened my mouth.

But this time, there was no way out. My boss had picked me, despite knowing full well how I struggled with **articulation** while my colleagues were far more fluent. Anger simmered within me. Why did my boss pick me? Each night, I tossed and turned. My hands gripped the sheets my mind racing with thoughts of failure. What if I embarrassed myself and the presentation **ruined** my chance for a promotion, or worse cost my job?

Seeking Guidance

In search of guidance and reassurance, I called my uncle back in Kenya. As a well-known tribal leader and speaker, his words carried weight. His advice was unconventional:

"My son, on the big day of presentation, **oil your buttocks for good luck,**" he said.

"Really?" I asked, letting his words sink in. A small part of me wondered if there was more to this bizarre tradition than met the eye.

"I do that all the time," he replied with surety.

I laughed at the absurdity, but it was the touch of humor I needed to break the tension. Yet, I knew humor alone wouldn't suffice. I needed more practical solutions. Still, the **odd advice** lingered in the back of my mind—curious, tempting, almost daring me to test its power when the moment came. They say a desperate man will cling to a knife. The option for lotion seemed easier. Could a little **superstition** really tip the scales in my favor?

Finding Solutions

Desperate to combat my **glossophobia**, I searched the internet for solutions. I watched posture videos and practiced controlled breathing. I expanded my vocabulary by making up 20 words from each letter of the alphabet. This exercise improved my language skills and boosted my **confidence.**

I practiced in front of mirrors to build my confidence. Each time I stood in front of the mirror, my reflection stared back. At first, it felt awkward, like I was staring at all **my life's failures.** I knew I could run and hide or face the guy in the mirror. I chose to face him. I had to accept and embrace my accent.

As Criss Jami said, "To share your **weakness** is to make yourself vulnerable; to make yourself vulnerable is to show your strength." This acceptance brought a small yet significant relief. Understanding that my accent was an inseparable part of me, I felt a profound sense of peace. My shoulders relaxed, and my voice steadied as I embraced my true self.

The Big Day

As the presentation day neared, my **anxiety intensified**. I whispered, "Lord, do your thing; I've done my part," but it felt like I was sending God an email. On the day of the presentation, my heart pounded, and my hands trembled as if gripped by an invisible force. I felt utterly alone. Moments before stepping onto the stage, my boss's firm hand on my shoulder and a few kind words ignited a spark of confidence.

For the first time, I felt hopeful, though I was oily and nervous. Maybe I could do this; maybe I wouldn't fail. It was a flicker, delicate and fleeting but its impact undeniable. With shaky legs, a nervous voice, and a churning stomach, I climbed onto the stage, clutching a small plastic bag in my pocket just in case I **vomited.**

The room felt stifling. Each gaze bored into me, stripping away my confidence piece by piece. The silence amplified the sound of my heartbeat in my ears. I stumbled over the opening lines, sweat dripping down my spine. Avoiding the audience's eyes, I focused on the exit as if my ancestors might appear in a puff of smoke to whisk me away from this ordeal.

After a **painful 15 minutes of torture**, murmurs of encouragement reached me. Then, something shifted. I noticed a few words, a few smiles. Slowly, I felt less like an **imposter** and more like a storyteller finding my faint voice. Each word was a battle against the glossophobia threatening to **paralyze me.**

Transformation and Growth

To my astonishment, the room erupted with subtle applause as I finished. Maybe it was merciful applause. Perhaps they just couldn't wait for me to conclude my speech. But at that moment, as relief settled in like a cool breeze, I realized my fears were unfounded. The audience celebrated my unique accent, **embracing** me for who I was. Their support turned my dread into empowerment.

With newfound **confidence** and my boss's encouragement, we started a public speaking club at our company. I embraced every opportunity to speak. Even as more **intimidating** fears surfaced, I refused to let them stop me. Each speech helped shed old fears and gain new assurance.

Winning several speech contests, I felt like stepping into a new world. It wasn't just about the trophies; it was about conquering the fear that had once paralyzed me. With each victory, I felt a surge of pride and a growing belief in my own capabilities.

Embracing Humor

Later, I called my uncle to thank him for his advice. He asked, "So, did you oil your buttons?"

I paused, baffled. **"What buttons?"**

"You know, the ones on your clothes," he clarified as if it was the most obvious thing in the world.

We both burst into laughter. The misunderstanding had turned a nerve-wracking situation into a shared joke, dissolving the tension. Moving forward, I knew I wouldn't take his advice so literally. Whatever **rituals help** you get on stage, go for it—just make sure they actually work for you!

Embracing Potential

Confronting glossophobia **unlocked** my potential for creativity and leadership, transforming fear into a gateway to opportunities. By stepping out of my comfort zone to speak at major conferences, I discovered that growth often stems from discomfort.

Once the pandemic hit, my triumph over glossophobia—a fear that had silenced me for years—gave me the courage to start creating short inspirational social media videos. I vividly remember the first few videos I posted—they went viral. I received heartfelt comments from people who felt **motivated** by my message. But there were **hate messages** too—people mocking my voice or dismissing my story. It was a reminder that speaking out meant standing tall in the face of both **praise and criticism**. I realized that my voice—**imperfect** as it was—still had the power to resonate.

Reflecting on my journey, I understand that my voice holds immense value, and my story deserves to be heard. Embracing and accepting my shortcomings have distinguished me from others. Remember, **opportunity** often meets you at your readiness—be prepared to seize it.

Encouragement for Your Journey

If you've already started the journey of public speaking, realize that growth is uncomfortable—it signifies progress. Yes, you can—just as I have. Remember, you are the **greatest project** you'll ever work on. Embrace each opportunity to speak to different audiences, and watch yourself transform with every experience.

Restart. **Reset**. Refocus. Reinvent as many times as you need. Just don't give up. Imagine stepping off the stage, having conquered glossophobia, your voice finally heard and new opportunities awaiting you. As my uncle once advised, sometimes all you need is a little humor to get through tough times. Do you need some oil to help you glide through your next bout of glossophobia?

The Grace of Plain Cassava: A Daily Ritual

The Drought

During my childhood in Kenya, a severe drought **devastated** our land, turning fertile fields into cracked earth. All that remained was **cassava**—its starchy roots a bitter comfort as the **drought** claimed our cattle and every vegetable in our gardens. Shared meals bound us together in desperate scarcity. The thin, strained laughter of elders tried to mask the reality. **Anguish** seeped into everything. The children's cries still echoed through the village, haunting reminders of all we had lost.

Prayers and Hunger

The village witch doctor intensified his fervent prayers for rain. Our empty stomachs echoed in pleas. Yet, in this simplicity, a

163

profound lesson emerged through a **new daily ritual** my father initiated. Each morning, with a piece of cassava in hand, we'd point towards the **shuttered butchery,** a symbol of the meat we longed for but no longer had.

At first, I thought hunger had driven my father crazy, but he reminded us, "Keep pointing for the next generation." As I bit into the plain cassava, it tasted richer than I ever remembered—whether from **hunger** or the haze of desperation. This playful gesture of appreciating the meat we no longer had delighted the young ones, whose laughter cut through our despair. Soon, others followed. This ritual spread throughout the village. It sustained us during the drought, **planting seeds** for lifelong gratitude. Despite our **hardships**, this practice deepened our appreciation for what little remained.

Facing Skepticism and Conflict

Skepticism crept into our lives, both from within our family and from the village. The witch doctor, long respected and feared, accused my father of practicing **"cassava witchcraft."** To most of the villagers, his words carried weight; he had been a source of guidance for years, and his rituals were often seen as the village's lifeline.

One evening, as the sun dipped below the horizon, the witch doctor confronted my father in the village square.

"You are misleading our people," he declared, his voice filled with anger. "This pointing ritual is **blasphemy**. Only the gods can save us from this drought."

My father, calm but resolute, replied,

"I am not challenging the gods. I am teaching our children to find hope and gratitude in what we have, no matter how little."

164

But the witch doctor was not satisfied. He warned of divine **retribution** and sought to rally the villagers against my father. Fear rippled through the crowd; some whispered among themselves, uncertain whether to follow the man they had trusted for so long or the one who offered a new kind of hope.

Under this shadow, the **tension** between them escalated, dividing the village. Some feared the witch doctor's wrath, yet my father's unwavering belief inspired others in gratitude. Whispers spread, emboldened by those who shared his skepticism. The witch doctor demanded my father's punishment. But the village elders, their bodies and spirits weakened by hunger, refused to act.

At first, the villagers remained uncertain, torn between the witch doctor's warnings and my father's quiet resolve. Yet, as days passed and the drought persisted, their faith in old rituals began to wane. My father's message of gratitude, though simple, started to resonate with those who had grown weary of fear.

This moment marked a **turning point**. Justice was served. What began as whispers of doubt turned into quiet conversations around evening fires, and soon, the villagers began to see the wisdom in my father's words. A change was in the air. Slowly, the village began to adopt my father's **perspective**, finding strength in gratitude rather than fear. People started forming small groups early in the morning to point their pieces of cassavas at the **butchery** together, turning a solitary act into a shared ritual of hope. It felt like a church without walls.

Daily Gratitude Practice

Despite the **witch doctor's threats**, my father showed us that gratitude isn't just for special days; it's a **daily practice** that brings light to our darkest moments. As Amy Weatherly once said, "Some people could be given an entire field of roses and only see thorns in it. Others could be given a single weed and only see the wildflower in it." This wisdom, born from hardship, emphasized the universal nature of gratitude.

Modernizing the Ritual

Inspired by this lesson, I've woven our pointing ritual into the fabric of my daily life. Each morning, my phone and **Outlook calendar** gently remind me to reflect on my blessings with simple affirmations: "I'm blessed. I'm thankful for another day," and "I'm healthy and wealthy." Just as we pointed to what we lacked, I now point to what I have. These reminders have become my anchors, grounding me no matter the storm. They have transformed the way I navigate challenges, always with gratitude in mind.

One vivid example stands out. I was in a car accident. The sound of crunching metal and shattering glass filled the air as I braced myself for the worst. After the initial shock, my friend called to check on me. My first words were, **"Thank God I'm okay,** and I can afford a car." In that moment, amidst the chaos, my gratitude practice shone through, transforming a potentially distressing experience into one of profound appreciation.

It reminded me of those days when **cassava was all we had**— bitter comfort in hard times. Yet, just like then, I found something to be grateful for.

This **modern adaptation** ensures the essence of our tradition thrives in contemporary life. Each reminder is more than a habit; it's a lifeline that nurtures my soul, a daily affirmation of the good that surrounds me, no matter the circumstances. Despite the hustle and bustle of modern life, this ritual keeps me **centered**, reminding me of the abundance I often overlook.

166

Full Circle of Gratitude

More than 20 years later, my relatives and I now own the only butchery in the village—now a major town. What was once a symbol of our longing during the drought has become a testament to our perseverance. Was it my father's "cassava witchcraft" or just the whims of luck? We may never know, but this blessing has certainly found its way back to us. Now, as we provide for our community, I realize we're not just selling meat—we're sharing a story of **survival** and the enduring **power of belief.**

Refocusing Through Gratitude

Research shows that practicing gratitude can enhance mental wellness and promote a lasting change in **perspective.** In our fast-paced world, taking a moment to appreciate what we have can significantly **alter our outlook,** affecting not only our personal lives but also those around us. By **training your mind** and heart to see the good in everything, you'll find there is always something to be thankful for—even a piece of cassava.

What is your grace pointing to today?

The Joy of Selfless Giving:
Embracing Joy without Expectations

Unexpected Challenges

Growing up in Kenya, we imagined every city in the US to be like New York, a vast mega hub bustling with cabs, buses, and trains. Influenced by **glossy urban** depictions in movies, my Indian friends arrived in Houston in early 2002, expecting a similarly reliable public transportation system. Reality? They encountered infrequent and unreliable buses.

They were shocked, asking, "You mean there are no trains or yellow cabs everywhere like in the movies?"

Seeing Akhil's disillusionment under the scorching sun I felt a surge of **empathy** as I recalled my own initial culture shock. As college mates, our shared experiences moved me to start driving them to school each morning on my way to work.

169

Embracing Mutual Aid

This routine embraced the spirit of my village's culture of mutual aid. Timeless. An inherent rhythm in every villager valued patience over punctuality. Embracing this spirit, I gave them my old furniture as we were all struggling to get by. (Maybe the couch had seen better days, but it was free!)

A Harsh Lesson

One summer day, when **my car broke down**, and I called them for help.

"Sorry, we can't help you; we leave early," Akhil replied with his nasal voice.

"I'll wake up early if I need to," I answered, hopeful.

"I'm sorry, we don't want to divert our route," he replied.

There was an awkward pause; you could cut the tension with an axe.

I was gutted. A heavy feeling of **betrayal** engulfed me. I gripped the phone, my hands trembling slightly, my voice cracking. I had to double-check the phone number; my brain refused to accept their rejection. How could they, after all the mornings, shielding them from **Houston's harsh weather** without ever charging them for gas or car repairs?

Memories of our warm, carefree days together flooded back, tainted by their refusal to help me now when I needed it most. Betrayal. The bonds of our friendship felt like a shattered vase, **pieces irreparably scattered.** I felt a hollow ache in my chest. I had to steady myself and sit on my living room couch, staring at the carpet for answers. At that moment, I realized that **trust,** once broken, is difficult to mend. The ache in my chest deepened as I wondered how to navigate this new reality.

Disappointment and Reflection

After venting enough, I dragged myself to the bus stop, heart heavy. The undependable bus rides and relentless humidity humbled me. This harsh lesson about the **fragility of expectations** led to a deeper understanding. Watching the varied expressions of fellow passengers, I realized genuine giving involves no expectations.

Were you disappointed when someone you helped said no to your request? Are you still holding a **grudge?**

Beyond Transactional Relationships

Reflecting on this experience, I began to understand a broader truth: some people help others with the expectation of favors in return. Their motivation is **transactional.** Have you ever encountered someone like this? If you ever help someone and can't reciprocate, be honest and prepare for potential **fallout.** Such individuals may gossip or tarnish your name if you can't reciprocate. Avoid this **trap** and move on with your life.

But remember, not everyone operates this way. Seek out and nurture relationships built on genuine care and mutual respect. These are the connections that will truly enrich your life. Helping others should come from a genuine intent, not from expecting something in return. When you learn to **accept instead of expect**, you'll experience fewer disappointments and find greater peace. True **generosity** is about giving without any strings attached.

The Power of Forgiveness

Life has a funny way of bringing people back into your life at the wrong time. Eventually, our paths crossed again at a friend's wedding. Seeing them, I felt irritated. Stoic. My mind raced with memories of **past betrayals** and the sting of their refusal. This was my moment to express my disappointment and make them feel guilty. Despite the resurfacing feelings of betrayal, I greeted them warmly. In that split second, I realized something important: holding onto anger would only weigh me down. I chose **peace over conflict.** My reaction said more about me than it did about them.

They hesitated, then shared the struggles they'd faced with their car, echoing my earlier role as their guide. Understanding their challenges, I forgave them. I realized their hesitation wasn't out of malice but mere oversight. As I reflected on this, it became clear that I don't have to **rebuild relationships** with everyone I have forgiven.

Is there someone who let you down? Someone you need to forgive without the burden of reconnection?

Embracing Joy in Giving

Life is too short. **Grudges** are a waste of perfect happiness. Apologize when you can and let go of what you can't. You have to take the good with the bad. Learn from your mistakes, but never regret them because people change and things go wrong. Life goes on.

Now, whenever I help someone, I remind myself: "I'm doing this because I want to, not because I have to." This mindset of releasing expectations has made my life more enjoyable and peaceful. It's a daily practice of embracing **life's unpredictability** and finding joy in the selflessness of giving, aligning with my deepest values.

Reflection and Growth

Reflect on a recent favor you've done. Did you find yourself hoping for something in return? Life's shifts and surprises aren't mere twists of fate—they're opportunities for growth. By giving without expecting back, we enhance our **capacity for happiness,** aligning our actions with meaningful intentions. These lessons extend beyond broken-down cars or bus rides—they are guiding principles for life.

A Prayer for Healing

I pray you find the strength to forgive those who have let you down. Just as I forgave my friends in Houston, release the burden of unspoken apologies and embrace the joy of selfless giving. Remember, unforgiveness is like **drinking poison** and expecting someone else to suffer.

May your journey be filled with genuine connections, deep satisfaction, and the lightness that comes with a heart unburdened by grudges.

From Women's Shoes to Self-Discovery:
Overcoming Cherophobia

The Beginning of the Shoe Venture

As a broke college student, I found myself dating a woman with an insatiable thirst for shoes—a stark contrast to my own thirst for money. She was a vision of timeless beauty, framed by cascades of silky hair that caught the light with every movement. She was **mesmerizing**. She made you forget your worries. The kind of woman I fell in love with and willingly sold all my ancestral land for.

She dragged me to her shoe-buying spree. **A price for love.** During the shoe sprees, I stumbled upon a lucrative opportunity: reselling discounted women's shoes from the local mall. This was when **eBay** was booming, and the timing seemed perfect. What began as a side hustle to ease our financial strain and cater to her passion quickly **consumed me.** The thrill of turning a profit and the growing success of the venture made it impossible to resist.

175

At first, the thrill of making profits was intoxicating, but a nagging fear lurked in the back of my mind, whispering that this happiness was too good to last. With every increase in profits, my anxiety grew, and the pressure to maintain the facade of success became almost unbearable.

The Strain on Relationships

Sleepless nights became the norm. I obsessed over the next big sale, my mind racing with anxiety. My grades began to slip, and my room turned into a chaotic sea of shoeboxes and packing slips. A reflection of the **turmoil within me**. Friends started to drift away, tired of my constant cancellations and distracted conversations.

"Dude, you're always busy," one of them remarked with evident frustration.

My girlfriend, once a **source of joy**, now became a silent observer of my decline. She tried to engage me in conversations, but my mind was always elsewhere, calculating profits and losses. One evening, as we sat in the dim light of our dining room, she turned to me, her eyes full of concern.

"You've changed," she said softly, poking the elephant in the room.

"This is all because of you," I yelled at her. "Your shoe addiction is killing me."

Her eyes widened in shock. "Me? Are you crazy? I've always supported you with your business," she retorted, her voice rising.

"Then stop it," I snapped, unable to control my frustration.

A heavy silence fell. She looked at me, **hurt** etched on her face, and I felt a pang of guilt. I knew I couldn't stop myself. I was **addicted** to the thrill of a sale and the looming anxiety of potential failure that followed.

The Turning Point

The day my **girlfriend left,** her parting words cut deeply:

"I can't live like this anymore; you care about your shoes more than me."

Her departure was not just a wake-up call—it was a **devastating** blow that revealed the full extent of my fears. My **cherophobia,** the fear of being happy, had driven a **wedge** between us. It made me believe that happiness was always just a precursor to loss.

As the door closed behind her, the ensuing silence was a stark reminder of this crippling fear. I felt lost, confused, and frustrated because I meant well but couldn't control this fear. The empty room echoed with memories of happier times, now tainted by my inability to hold on to them.

As I sat there in my quiet dining room with unsold shoes scattered on the floor, a surge of frustration welled up inside me.

"This is all because of you over there," I yelled at the shoes on the floor. "Stop staring at me! And you, **Tory Burch,** wipe that smirk off your face!"

My voice cracked the absurdity of my outburst, only highlighting my desperation. The silence that followed was deafening. The shoes, **lifeless** and indifferent, seemed to mock me with their silence. At that moment, I realized I was not just losing my girlfriend—I was **losing myself** to a fear that I had let rule my life.

Overwhelmed by a sense of loss and emptiness, I found **no joy** in my shoe business anymore. In a fit of anger, I donated all the shoes to a local charity, desperate to rid myself of the reminders of her and my **failures**. This painful moment forced me to confront my issues head-on. The loneliness and despair became unbearable, leading me to seek help.

Understanding Cherophobia

In my search for understanding, I discovered the term "cherophobia"—the fear of being happy. Cherophobia, though not widely discussed, is a real condition that can affect many aspects of one's life. It often stems from **past traumas,** such as childhood experiences where happiness leads to negative consequences.

Every moment of happiness felt like a delicate glass ornament, beautiful yet fragile, always at risk of shattering—a belief deeply rooted in my past. Since high school, we barely celebrated small **achievements,** whether it was a good grade on a test or a successful performance in a school play. Our parents always pushed us for greater accomplishments.

Their praise was fleeting, overshadowed by the next demand. It left us to wonder if anything we did was ever enough. The **constant pressure** overshadowed our pride, deepening my fear that joy was fleeting and perilous. It was this fear that entrenched my cherophobia, casting a shadow over even the brightest moments.

Recognizing these patterns helped me see that my feelings were not just personal but part of a **broader psychological issue** shared by many. Understanding cherophobia's roots and manifestations can be the first step toward overcoming it. It allows individuals to reclaim their right to happiness.

A Grandmother's Wisdom

One evening, I called my grandmother back home, a woman who had weathered many storms with quiet strength. She listened patiently as I poured out my heart. After a long pause, she began to speak, her voice steady and comforting.

"In the old days, we would **scribble markings on trees** or big rocks after a successful event, like a big harvest. Those markings reminded us of our achievements and gave us **hope**, especially during tough times."

"You should do something similar."

"You want me to start scribbling on random trees?" I inquired.

"No, silly, get a **jar** and write down all your **past successes.** Fill the jar with these notes, and let them remind you of your strength and resilience. Fill your life with experiences, not things. Have stories to tell, not things to show."

Her words were simple yet profound, carrying the weight of generations of wisdom. I felt a knot in my chest loosen.

"You deserve happiness, even if you're not used to it."

As I hung up, her words echoed in my mind. **Simple,** yet powerful. For the first time in a long while, I felt a glimmer of hope.

The Healing Process

Though initially, the jar's simplicity seemed too modest to tackle my complex fears, her encouragement to "look beyond the jar" revealed its deeper significance. This simple act began to bridge the gap between my fears and the life I wanted to reclaim. As I placed the first note in the jar, a mix of **skepticism** and curiosity washed over me. The paper felt insignificant in my hands, yet heavy with meaning. I remember staring at the jar afterwards, feeling a subtle shift inside— a spark of hope amidst the doubt.

This act, as minor as it seemed, **cracked** the veneer of my cherophobia. Each note became a **beacon,** a small reminder that happiness didn't have to be feared but embraced. Every time those doubts crept into my mind, my **trusty jar** was awaiting positive reminders.

A New Beginning

Each time I read those notes, I felt hopeful and powerful. Filling the jar shifted my skepticism to belief. It didn't just change my view on happiness; it changed how I interacted with the world. This was a **powerful shift**, a reminder of my worth, my presence, and my contribution to the world. I moved with a newfound energy, my steps light and my pace brisk. My friends noticed the change. I was no longer paralyzed by the **fear of happiness** turning into sorrow but invigorated by the possibility of joy.

Though my girlfriend never returned, I found **peace** in the changes I had made. Initially, her departure left me devastated, but focusing on my jar helped me rediscover my strength. I quit the shoe business and sent the remainder to Grandma.

My jar continued to fill with victories, each note a testament to my resilience and growth. Each small note—"first successful shoe business," "Gifted grandma her first pair of Prada"—helped build a foundation of confidence and happiness I never imagined I'd find again.

Conclusion

Reflecting on this journey, I realize that each small note built a foundation of confidence and happiness that once seemed unattainable. This realization compels me to encourage others: If you're suffering from cherophobia—always feeling like something bad is about to happen when something good occurs, or if you ever feel like you don't deserve anything good, consider starting your own jar. A simple jar filled with **personal victories** can profoundly change your life.

As Nishan Panwar once said, "If you live in fear of the future because of what happened in your past, you'll end up losing what you have in the present."

Trust the process. Trust your intuition. **Trust yourself.** Happiness is not something to fear but something to embrace—because you deserve to live fully, not just survive.

Summary:

Through these stories, we witness the transformative power of facing glossophobia, embracing gratitude, giving without expectations, and confronting cherophobia. Each narrative highlights the essence of **personal growth and resilience,** showing us how overcoming these challenges leads to a richer, more courageous life. Ultimately, these stories inspire us to live fully and fearlessly, embracing every obstacle as a stepping stone to a brighter future.

Part VIII: Finding Joy and Balance in Life

Explore stories of commitment, resilience, and redefining home. Discover how facing challenges with determination transforms setbacks into lessons, leading to personal growth and a deeper sense of belonging. Embrace the journey to find joy and balance in life.

"A change in bad habits leads to a change in life."
– Jenny Craig

Soccer Boots and Leather Goods: A Commitment Device

In my Kenyan village, **Uncle Mbiti,** aptly named **"Hyena,"** ran our family's leather factory. After every small business success, he'd vanish for days, slipping away like the cunning hyena on the prowl. Gone. No one knew where he went or when he'd return. But when he did, he returned with stories—captivating tales of outwitting rival traders in distant markets and **bold ventures** through treacherous terrain to find the finest hides. His wallet was usually empty by the time he got home—a testament to the life he led: thrilling, **unpredictable,** unforgettable.

Despite producing high-quality leather goods—from belts to soccer balls—the factory's success was as unpredictable as a hyena's hunt. It thrived or faltered on the whims of the local villagers' cowhides. They couldn't afford transportation to the big city factories, so they walked—miles. Clad in vibrant shukas, they trudged to Uncle Mbiti, their hopes growing heavier with each weary step—all pinned on his **success.**

The Power of Distraction

One day, a large order from a city client presented a big opportunity. However, Uncle Mbiti, swept up in nostalgia for his soccer days, **nearly missed it**. Alongside his friends, all former soccer enthusiasts, he momentarily put aside the pressing needs of the business, **risking** the factory's future. You'd think the **World Cup** was happening right in our backyard the way they carried on. This moment underscored the powerful **pull of distractions**, particularly when they connect us to cherished pastimes.

Ultimatum

My grandfather, weary of his antics, gave a stern ultimatum: "Focus on the business or lose your job."

Uncle Mbiti felt immense pressure immediately. Filled with a deep sense of loss, he handed his cherished soccer gear to Grandma. His worn-out boots, once a symbol of **joy and freedom**, now became a solemn reminder of his responsibilities.

This act served as his **commitment device,** a physical reminder of his dedication to the business. A commitment device is a deliberate action or decision that helps a person stick to their goals by limiting future choices or creating **incentives** for desired behavior.

Reflect on a time when distractions derailed your progress.

The Breaking Point

Frustration often peaked for Uncle Mbiti—machines breaking down, water pipes bursting, and orders being delayed. One particularly challenging day, as I brought him lunch, he stared longingly at his dusty soccer shorts, a reminder of simpler, happier times. Overwhelmed by a mix of anger, **sadness, and regret,** tears spilled over as he shouted,

"I can't take this anymore," into the empty factory.

His old soccer friends laughed at him for quitting, amplifying his sense of failure and **isolation**. Remember, pursuing important goals often brings guilt from those who once walked beside you. But have you ever found yourself **blaming** others for your own distractions?

A Renewed Commitment

But then, he remembered his grandfather's words: "Learn to rest, not to quit, when you get tired."

The commitment he had made echoed in his mind. Taking a deep breath, he decided to persevere. He focused on **small steps** to improve the situation, each task a tiny beacon of hope. He started sorting raw cowhides into sizes for chemical spray, the rough texture of hides grounding him in the present moment.

Learning from Uncle Mbiti's Sacrifices

Each glance at his old soccer boots reminded him of the **sacrifices** he was making and why they were necessary. Uncle Mbiti's life illustrates the power of distractions and the importance of taking responsibility for our own focus. Drawing inspiration from his journey, here are some practical steps to overcome distractions:

187

Steps to Overcome Distractions

- **Create a Commitment Device**: Just as Uncle Mbiti sacrificed his soccer boots, find a personal item or habit to give up or repurpose as a reminder of your commitment. This can help reinforce your focus and determination.

- **Use Time Blocking**: Schedule dedicated time blocks for important tasks to maintain concentration.

- **Set Daily Goals:** Simplify your workload and boost motivation by achieving small, manageable tasks each day.

- **Embrace Boredom:** Allow yourself periods of **boredom** to boost creativity and mental clarity. Sometimes, the mind needs a break from constant stimulation to reset and refocus.

The Triumph

After three months of tireless effort, Uncle Mbiti emerged from the factory, embodying the tenacity of his nickname. Despite the visible fatigue, his eyes sparkled with **triumph.** The client was so impressed that they paid him a bonus for completing the task ahead of schedule. This was more than a financial win; it was a personal triumph over the distractions and doubts that once threatened to derail him.

At that moment, he knew sacrificing his soccer boots had been worth it. Uncle Mbiti's victory secured his business's future and had a ripple effect throughout the community. This triumph **inspired** my grandfather to open a footwear design school, offering new opportunities to local students.

Creating a Legacy

As Uncle Mbiti watched the new hires, he saw not just the preservation of his family's legacy but also the creation of his own. This tale of focus and sacrifice underscores the importance of **prioritizing** what truly matters. Uncle Mbiti's decision didn't merely save his business; it also catalyzed community development, supporting educational initiatives and inspiring others. The factory became an option for local families who couldn't **afford** high school fees.

Now It's Your Turn: Reflect and Act

Reflect on this: Uncle Mbiti's journey teaches us that letting go of lesser dreams can lead to more fulfilling pursuits. Identify the distractions holding you back and the sacrifices you can make today to focus on what truly matters.

If you've allowed distraction to steal your purpose, don't be afraid to rise again. **To try again.** To love again. To live again. And to dream again. Don't let a hard lesson harden you. Use it as a stepping stone towards a more focused and fulfilling life.

By overcoming distractions and committing to your goals, you can build a legacy that transcends individual **achievements**. Follow these steps to achieve your goals and create a lasting impact, just as Uncle Mbiti did.

So what are your "soccer boots"? What distraction do you need to set aside to reclaim your purpose?

Savannah Milk and Cow Dung:
Resilience in the Heart of the Homestead

Mornings on the Savannah: Life at Dawn

Growing up in Kenya, my early mornings burst into life with the vibrant sounds and sights of dawn on the savannah. The sky would blush with the first light of day, a soft, pink glow. My grandmother's footsteps echoed down the cool stone hallway to the kitchen, the **heart of our home.**

Outside, our rooster's piercing crow cut through the morning haze while distant **hyenas laughed** under a rosy sky. Amidst the vast silence of the savannah, she began each day by **milking Kibuku**, our cow. Kibuku was a short-horned **Zebu breed** with a distinctive thoracic hump, a sloping rump, and rather long legs—often referred to as "humped cattle." She could've passed for a supermodel if cows modeled. Life was simple. We **parted cow thighs** for milk and murmured sweet nothings to goats. We wove whispers of joy into the

191

fabric of our days, and some days, my cousin and I would sneak and suck milk straight from the cow's udder. Risky, but pure bliss.

Lessons from the Cowshed: Resilience in Everyday Life

For the morning milking, I tied Kibuku's hind leg between two nearby trees. Nature seemed to have intended them for this very task. Yet, getting her out of the cowshed took extra effort on rainy days. I navigated the slippery dung in the cowshed—a cold and smelly dance of necessity. The **wet cow dung** smelled strongly of earth and decay. It reminded me of farm life's rawness.

On challenging days when Kibuku kicked over the **milk jug,** sending our efforts splashing into the dirt with a defiant mood, I felt a mix of frustration and admiration. Kibuku had her moments, like the time she chewed **Grandma's bra** right off the clothesline. I had to pull the bra from her mouth, stifling laughter at the absurdity of it all. Payback for all the times we pulled her away from chewing plastic paper. As the saying goes, **"Tit for tat is a fair game."**

Watching my grandmother handle these moments with serene resilience—her calm as steady as the dawn—instilled in me a deep sense of **stability** and strength. It was in these ridiculous moments that I realized life's lessons often come wrapped in humor. It also a reminded me that **cows don't give milk;** we have to work for it.

Seasonal Struggles: Embracing the Cycles of Life

Cleaning the cowshed and carrying the manure taught us the importance of patience and **diligence.** Just as our cow, Kibuku, faced the seasonal ebb and flow of milk production, so too did our neighbors' cows. They calved at different times of the year. This shared experience highlighted our seasonal dance, showing that the "cow dung" moments—**messy and inevitable**—were essential for **growth.** While navigating its own rhythm, each household silently acknowledged its part in a larger, shared cycle of resilience.

192

Who in your family has **inspired** your resilience, and how have their actions shaped the way you handle your own "cow dung" moments?

This realization that **struggles are seasonal**—that navigating through the mess to obtain the milk was temporary and came in waves—offered not just comfort but also a sense of community. Observing each family manage their seasons of **abundance and scarcity,** along with their communal support during calving and milking, reinforced a valuable lesson: Our challenges are both **temporary** and shared experiences.

Nourishing Resilience: Finding Strength in the Mess

In our life's cycle, we experience our own **Season of Expansion**, marked by growth, learning, and exploration. Like working in the cowshed, we navigate the cow dung of challenges, take risks, adapt to changes, and broaden our horizons. This is followed by the **Season of Mastery**, where we harvest the milk of our efforts, deepen our expertise, refine our skills, and find stability and consistency in our pursuits. We earn our rewards.

Understanding these seasons helps us see our struggles and triumphs as part of a natural rhythm, providing **reassurance** that both abundance and scarcity are fleeting yet essential phases of growth.

Some generations may expect milk to flow **freely.** Some may even want to suck milk straight from the cow's udder. But let's be the ones who teach them to part cow thighs gently, **embrace** the muddy cowshed, persevere when the jug spills or when the cow kicks, and even pull their foot out of the cow dung. It's all part of the process. Above all, to try again. By doing so, we foster resilience, responsibility, and an indomitable spirit in ourselves and others. This prepares us not just for daily challenges but for life's broader journey.

Reflect on your own "cow dung moments." What season of life are you in?

193

Embodying the spirit of "Savannah Milk" means viewing each challenge as a season of growth, transforming **obstacles** into opportunities for strength. Let it guide us, nourishing our resilience and dedication to a hopeful future.

Every day, I remind myself that the life I have now was something I prayed for. Even with all the challenges and confusion, I asked to get this far. I wished for all this. This understanding of the cyclical nature of challenges not only reassures us but also binds us to a shared human experience.

Conclusion: Celebrating the Journey

Take a moment. Sit back. **Marvel at your life**—the grief that softened you, the heartaches that made you wiser, the suffering that strengthened you. Despite everything, you still grow. Just like the careful process of milking Kibuku, every effort and every challenge nourishes your spirit. Embrace the spirit of resilience. Together, we can transform obstacles into **stepping stones** for a hopeful future. Resilience and growth often spring from life's messiest moments.

Have you thanked yourself lately for making it this far in life? If not, do it now. Celebrate your journey and the strength you've gained along the way.

"Home is not where you live, but where they understand you."

Returning to the Roots:
Redefining Home

Homecoming in a Changed World

After more than 15 years in the US, the late 2000s brought me a chance to return to **Kenya**—a dream finally becoming reality. Boarding the plane, I felt like the **village's prodigal son**, carrying with me the weight of years spent away and the hope of **reconnecting** with my roots.

But as I stepped onto the plane, there was no elegant air hostess with a warm smile and a neatly tied neckerchief to greet me. Instead, a hurried "Hi, watch your step," barely lifted above the noise of boarding. The **journey home** had begun, but it was already clear that time had altered not just places, but the very essence of what "home" meant.

As the plane ascended, a mix of excitement and apprehension filled me. The hum of the engines seemed to echo the **questions** racing in my mind. I wondered how much had changed and how much of the Kenya I remembered would still be there.

Immediate Changes upon Arrival

The changes were immediate once I landed. An interaction over overweight luggage—a quiet dollar exchange—hinted at the **adaptations** and compromises ahead. Stepping outside, the air was cleaner and crisp, a refreshing change from the thick humidity of Houston. Even the world around me felt more compact, the **vastness of Texas** now a distant memory, replaced by the intimate, familiar scale of home.

The scent of fresh earth and blooming flowers mingled with faint hints of diesel from nearby taxis. The sound of **Swahili chatter** and the vibrant colors of **kanga fabric** reminded me of the vibrant life that awaited. Each breath felt like a homecoming, yet I couldn't help but feel a **pang of nostalgia** for the memories—a Kenya where every face was familiar, and every street felt like part of me.

Familiar sights now seemed distant, and once-warm glances felt tinged with estrangement. The beautiful **silky oak trees**, once a dominant feature of the landscape, now fought for space among new structures, their canopies a testament to resilience—much like me, struggling to reconcile the past with this transformed present, trying to find my place in this new world.

A Journey through Time

Driving to my village, Nguluni, felt like traveling through time. The wild savannah was now replaced by homes and developments, starkly contrasting my memories of open fields and rustic pathways. I could almost see the **ghost of my younger self** running through those fields, now buried beneath concrete. The once tranquil scenery filled with **gazelles** and buffaloes was now interrupted by bustling activity.

Returning to my village, the vibrancy of my childhood **clashed** with the present reality. The quiet, small village I remembered had transformed into a major city, bustling with business and a tripled population. As I navigated the crowded streets, I felt a **mix of awe and loss,** watching the new structures squeeze in around my grandmother's house as if trying to erase my very roots.

As we drove through the newly paved streets, the chatter of vendors and the hum of motorcycles replaced the silence of my youth. **Newcomers** from other tribes had settled in, introducing diverse cultures and dialects, adding both richness and complexity to the village's identity.

Uncle Mbiti's **leather factory** was now a church, reflecting the community's new needs and priorities. The change was inevitable. It felt as if the very fabric of my memories was being altered by the passage of time. Amidst all this transformation, I searched for something familiar, **a tether to the past**, but the landscape I once knew had shifted irreversibly.

Missing Traditions and Lost Connections

As I walked further, the absence of my grandmother and her cherished traditions, such as the milk greeting and **ostrich egg cake**, left a void. Her presence had been a cornerstone of my identity, and her absence now felt like a missing piece of my soul. A wave of **sorrow** enveloped me. The **urban noise** now muted the village's natural chorus of birds and insects, a constant background that once brought me comfort.

My fluent tribal dialect, once met with nods of recognition, sparked hushed **gossip**. Conversations that once flowed easily now felt strained and fragmented. The streets that once echoed with familiar laughter now felt foreign and distant. Even the trees in the market that my granddad planted had **vanished**, replaced by bustling iron-sheet vegetable stalls bustling with activity. I felt **a pang of loss** for the simpler, more connected times of my childhood.

New Faces, Old Memories

Surrounded by young **relatives** I had never met, I felt the weight of years in their curious faces. Each step was a journey through time, each memory **clashing** with the present reality. Under the **acacia tree** I planted at the age of ten, now towering above us, we shared a meal. The tree, with its canopy and deep roots, stood as a silent witness to time's passage, a symbol of growth and continuity. As we shared dishes of **sukuma wiki** and **ugali,** our conversation danced around the years I had been away, revealing the distance time had etched between us.

Bridging the Cultural Divide

As we sat in its shade, the scent of the freshly cooked sukuma wiki and ugali mingled with the earthy aroma of the tree's leaves. The silence between us was profound, filled with hesitant yet meaningful exchanges. An elder, trying to bridge the gap with humor, quipped,

"Do you own camels, goats, and cows in America?" His jest underscored the chasm of **misunderstanding** about my life abroad.

I smiled, but it felt hollow. The gap between our worlds seemed insurmountable, filled with **misconceptions** and half-understood realities. I was seen as the lucky one who made it to America, yet they couldn't grasp the struggle of being a **stranger** in your own home.

After the meal, I found myself sitting with some of my cousins around a crackling fire, the flames casting dancing shadows on our faces. The scent of spices from the meal still lingered in the air. I shared stories from my life in America, describing **the hustle and bustle** of city life and the constant pressure to succeed. They listened with wide eyes, but their question,

"Isn't everyone rich in America?" revealed how little they could truly understand.

"Not all," I explained. "Life in the city is expensive and challenging. Many people struggle just to make ends meet." I sighed, realizing how pervasive the myths about American life were.

Another cousin leaned forward, his eyes reflecting the firelight. "But what about all the big houses and **fancy cars** we see on TV?" he asked.

I shook my head, a small smile on my lips. "Those things exist, but they're not the whole story. There's a lot of stress and expectations. It's not as easy as it looks."

The fire crackled, and a thoughtful silence settled over us. **"The struggle was real,"** I thought, feeling the weight of the duality in my identity. Here I was, straddling two worlds that seemed to grow further apart with each passing year.

Reflections and Identity

Standing by Marcus's grave, the finality of his loss brought my reflections into sharp focus. The **somber rows of headstones** reminded me of my grandparents and my father's graves, each a stark symbol of absence and enduring love. I understood why **Marcus** nicknamed himself **"Halfrican American."** The duality of my existence became more apparent with each interaction. It was a poignant reminder of the worlds I straddled and the distances that grew between us.

I realized how much our lives had diverged and how **alien** my experiences had become to them. The profound sadness that accompanied those realizations felt **grounding**. As I stood amidst the silent reminders of lives lived and lost, I couldn't help but wonder: "Where would my own journey end?" Would it be in America, my adopted home, or in the village where my roots began?

Have you ever wondered where **you'd be laid to rest** when the time comes?

A Gift of Blessings

Later, my aunt approached me with a gift. "My son, here is a live chicken for you to take back to America." I grabbed the chicken with one hand, its feathers rustling gently.

She continued, "Don't forget to bring back her chicks."

I was touched by her gesture, a symbol of continuity and connection between my past and my present. This simple act encapsulated the blending of my **two worlds**, highlighting the ongoing ties to my roots despite the distance.

The Acacia Tree: A Symbol of Growth

Standing once more under the acacia tree, I closed my eyes and breathed deeply, feeling the warmth of the sun and the whisper of the wind through its branches. At this moment, **I felt truly planted.** This tree, like my journey, had weathered the seasons, grown resilient, and stood as a testament to time and change.

Redefining Home and Belonging

Home, I realized, is not just a **physical place** but a state of being—a tapestry woven from the relationships we nurture, the memories we cherish, and the inner peace we cultivate through **acceptance and forgiveness**. It is where our roots run deep, connecting us to our past. It allows us to grow into our future strengthened by the lessons of where we've been and inspired by the **possibilities** ahead. I felt a sense of peace, knowing I could carry the essence of home within me, no matter where I was.

I invite you to find your own place of solace and reflection. **Redefine "home"** as more than just a location but as a sanctuary of the heart where you find peace and belonging. Have you visited your "home" lately?

Summary:

Embracing life's challenges and lessons is a journey of growth and self-discovery, guiding us toward our true home. The stories in this section highlight the importance of facing difficulties with courage and an open mind. Setbacks and obstacles become valuable teachers, offering insights for personal development. These narratives reveal the power of resilience, adaptability, and a positive mindset. Additionally, we explore the concept of "home"—a state of being where we find comfort, belonging, and peace. Through these insights, we learn to see challenges as stepping stones to a richer, more enlightened life and discover what "home" truly means.

Closing

You are alive today for a purpose. **Today is no accident;** it's an opportunity. **Your aspirations and dreams remain within reach.** Your potential is vibrant, your talents undiminished, your inner truth untarnished—even if it has been hidden.

My life isn't perfect, but I've learned challenges and struggles are part of life. There were times when I doubted my path, when my dreams seemed distant, and my **strengths felt diminished.** But through perseverance, I discovered that every setback was a setup for a comeback. I'm still learning as I evolve, embracing each lesson along the way.

If you've missed a chance to showcase **your gifts**, know that your **life's canvas is wide** and waiting for new brushstrokes. Each day is a fresh start, a chance to redefine your journey and embrace your true self.

Thank you for choosing to join me on this journey by purchasing this book. Your support means the world to me, and I hope that the words within these pages have inspired you to step into the infinite possibilities that await you.

Embrace this knowledge, and step into the **Limited Horizons** that await you. You embody all that you wish to be. Remember, you can't give your life more time, so give the time you have more life.

About the Author

Wilhelm Macmay Mwengi's journey from the heart of Kenya to becoming a beacon of resilience in Texas is a testament to the strength of the human spirit. Overcoming a near-fatal biking accident and the daunting responsibility of caring for a paralyzed mother, an autistic nephew, and his two young daughters, Wilhelm transformed personal trials into triumphs. His journey of self-recovery led him to become a life coach and public speaking coach, an inspiring speaker, and a star on social media, where he connects with professionals and shares insights into resilience, public speaking, and personal growth. Today, Wilhelm is dedicated to helping others find their voice and reclaim their lives, embodying the power of overcoming adversity.